YOUR recipe could appear in our next cookbook!

Share your tried & true family favorites with us instantly at
www.gooseberrypatch.com
If you'd rather jot 'em down by hand, just mail this form to...
Gooseberry Patch • Cookbooks – Call for Recipes
PO Box 812 • Columbus, OH 43216-0812

If your recipe is selected for a book, you'll receive a FREE copy!

Please share only your original recipes or those that you have made your own over the years.

Recipe Name:

Number of Servings:

Any fond memories about this recipe? Special touches you like to add
or handy shortcuts?

Ingredients (include specific measurements):

Instructions (continue on back if needed):

Special Code: **cookbookspage**

Over

Extra space for recipe if needed:

Tell us about yourself...

Your complete contact information is needed so that we can send you your FREE cookbook, if your recipe is published. Phone numbers and email addresses are kept private and will only be used if we have questions about your recipe.

Name:

Address:

City: State: Zip:

Email:

Daytime Phone:

Thank you! Vickie & Jo Ann

CLASSIC
CROCKPOT
RECIPES

245 comforting family-favorite recipes for
everyday meals and special occasions.

Gooseberry Patch

An imprint of
The Globe Pequot Publishing Group, Inc.
64 South Main Street
Essex, CT 06426

www.gooseberrypatch.com

1•800•854•6673

Copyright 2024, Gooseberry Patch 978-1-62093-583-5

Do you have a tried & true recipe...

tip, craft or memory that you'd like to see featured in a **Gooseberry Patch** cookbook? Visit our website at **www.gooseberrypatch.com** and follow the easy steps to submit your favorite family recipe. Or send them to us at:

Gooseberry Patch
PO Box 812
Columbus, OH 43216-0812

Don't forget to include the number of servings your recipe makes, plus your name, address, phone number and email address. If we select your recipe, your name will appear right along with it... and you'll receive a **FREE** copy of the book!

CONTENTS

Dedication

To everyone who loves good home-cooked comfort food, shared with family & friends.

Appreciation

Thanks to all of you who shared your families' most delicious slow-cooked recipes with us!

HOT & TASTY BREAKFASTS

Pecan Brunch Dessert Casserole

Beckie Apple
Grannis, AR

I made this scrumptious dessert breakfast casserole for the first time over 25 years ago, when my mom and dad came to visit us. We all loved it! My parents are no longer with us, but Mom told me many times how she loved it.

1/4 c. butter, melted
1 loaf French bread, cut into
    2-inch cubes
4 eggs, beaten
2-1/4 c. whole milk
1 c. sugar

3/4 c. brown sugar, packed
1 T. vanilla extract
1 t. cinnamon
1/4 c. chilled butter, diced
1/2 c. chopped pecans

Set a 4-quart crockpot to medium or low setting. Add melted butter and bread cubes; set aside. Combine eggs, milk, sugars, vanilla and cinnamon in a large bowl; beat until frothy. Pour egg mixture evenly over bread cubes. Cover and continue cooking on medium setting for 1-1/2 to 2 hours, or on low setting for 3 to 4 hours, until set. Uncover; scatter diced butter and pecans on top. Cover and cook another 35 minutes. Serves 6 to 8.

A crockpot brunch is so versatile! Perfect for so many delightful occasions...Christmas morning, Easter sunrise, tailgating, kiddie sleepovers. Fill up the crock, then set the table, start the coffee pot and greet your guests with a smile.

HOT & TASTY BREAKFASTS

Blueberry-Cinnamon Bake
Diana Chaney
Olathe, KS

I make this recipe whenever I have overnight guests.
They're warm, ooey-gooey and delicious!

2 12.4-oz. tubes refrigerated
   cinnamon rolls
6-oz. container fresh blueberries
4 eggs, lightly beaten

1/2 c. milk
1 T. cinnamon
1 t. vanilla extract

Cut each cinnamon roll into 8 pieces; return icing packages to the refrigerator. Layer roll pieces in a 4-quart crockpot coated with non-stick vegetable spray. Scatter blueberries evenly over rolls; set aside. In a bowl, whisk together remaining ingredients; spoon over blueberries in crock. Cover and cook on high setting for 2 hours, or until rolls are set. Drizzle with reserved icing; serve warm. Makes 12 servings.

Mix up your own French vanilla coffee creamer...scrumptious!
In a one-quart canning jar, combine a 14-ounce can
sweetened condensed milk, 1-1/2 cups whole milk and
2 teaspoons vanilla extract. Cover and shake well;
shake again each time it's served. Keep refrigerated.

CLASSIC CROCKPOT RECIPES

Peaches & Cream Oatmeal
Mary Hughes
Talladega, AL

What a delight to have this oatmeal ready when everyone gets up in the morning! I like to use the old-fashioned canned "freestone" peaches when I can find them.

2 c. whole milk
1 c. steel-cut oats, uncooked
1 c. sliced peaches in light syrup,
    drained and diced
1/2 c. chopped walnuts or pecans
2 T. honey

2 T. light brown sugar, packed
1 T. butter, sliced
1/2 t. cinnamon
1/4 t. salt
Garnish: additional milk,
    brown sugar

In a lightly greased 4-quart crockpot, lightly mix together all ingredients except garnish. Cover and cook on low setting for 4 to 6 hours, checking after 4 hours. Garnish as desired. Serves 6 to 8.

Amie's Apple Oatmeal
Judy Taylor
Butler, MO

This recipe was given to me by my daughter. It's especially good in wintertime, made just as we like it. I have made some additions to suit our taste. For the liquid, use all or a combination of milk, water, half-and-half or flavored coffee creamer...total liquid used should be 4-1/2 cups. I recommend using a crockpot liner.

2 apples, peeled, cored and
    finely chopped
1 c. steel-cut oats, uncooked
2 t. cinnamon

Optional: 2 T. brown sugar,
    packed
4-1/2 c. milk or water

Combine all ingredients in a 4-quart crockpot. Cover and cook on low setting for 5 to 6 hours, until thickened. Makes 8 to 10 servings.

When you rise in the morning, form a resolution to
make the day a happy one for a fellow creature.
– Sydney Smith

HOT & TASTY BREAKFASTS

Tailgate Breakfast Casserole
Carol Lytle
Columbus, OH

On football weekends, this is a must! I put it together the night before, then in the morning it's hot and ready for our tailgate friends. Sometimes I'll give it a little heat with Mexican-blend cheese or a spoonful of diced chiles. Go team!

30-oz. pkg. frozen diced potatoes
    with onions & peppers,
    divided
2 8-oz. pkgs. shredded Colby
    Jack cheese, divided
1 lb. ground pork breakfast
    sausage, browned
    and drained, divided

2 t. garlic powder
salt and pepper to taste
8 eggs
2 c. milk

In a greased 6-quart crockpot, evenly layer 1/2 each of potatoes, cheese and browned sausage. Repeat layering; sprinkle with seasonings. Beat eggs in a large bowl. Whisk in milk; pour over ingredients in crock and mix gently. Cover and cook on low setting for 7 to 8 hours, until set. Makes 8 to 10 servings.

Crockpots are so handy, you may want more than one!
A 4 to 6-quart model is just right for families and
potlucks...a smaller 3-quart crockpot is perfect
for gravies, dips and sauces.

CLASSIC CROCKPOT RECIPES

Company Scrambled Eggs
Sharon Tillman
Hampton, VA

Such an easy way to fix scrambled eggs for a crowd! The red pepper and green onions make it perfect for a crafting brunch with friends. Change it up with crispy crumbled bacon instead of ham.

2 doz. eggs	1 T. butter
1 c. half-and-half	1/2 c. red pepper, diced
1/2 t. salt	1/2 c. green onions, diced
1/2 t. pepper	1 c. shredded Cheddar cheese
2 c. cooked ham, diced	

Spray a 5-quart crockpot with non-stick vegetable spray. Add eggs to crock; beat well with an electric mixer on medium speed. Beat in half-and-half, salt and pepper until smooth. Sprinkle ham on top. Cover and cook on high setting for one hour, stirring after 30 minutes. Cover and cook another 40 to 50 minutes longer, stirring every 10 minutes, until eggs are nearly set. Meanwhile, melt butter in a skillet over medium heat. Add red pepper and onions; cook for 5 minutes, stirring occasionally, until pepper is tender. Fold pepper mixture and cheese into eggs. Serve right away, or turn crock to low setting and hold up to one hour. Serves 10 to 12.

Serve up stacks of hot toast with egg dishes...easy! Preheat the oven to 350 degrees. Arrange bread slices in a single layer directly on a lower oven rack. Bake for 4 minutes; turn over and bake another 3 to 4 minutes, until crisp and golden.

HOT & TASTY BREAKFASTS

Easy Cheesy Grits

Zoe Bennett
Columbia, SC

A must on brunch buffets down south! I like to serve these grits garnished simply, with chopped ripe tomatoes and green onions, or fancied up with sautéed shrimp and crispy bacon. Be sure to choose stone-ground grits, not instant or quick-cook grits...they'll cook up tender and delicious in your crockpot.

1-1/2 c. stone-ground
   grits, uncooked
6 c. chicken broth or water
1/2 t. onion powder
1/2 t. garlic powder

salt to taste
8-oz. pkg. shredded sharp
   Cheddar or Pepper
   Jack cheese

In a 6-quart crockpot, combine grits, chicken broth and seasonings; mix well. Cover and cook on low setting for 6 to 7 hours, until grits are tender. Stir in cheese until melted and serve. Makes 8 servings.

Cook bacon with less spattering! Just add 3 or 4 tablespoons of water to the cold skillet as you add the bacon slices. Cook as usual. You'll get crisp bacon without the mess.

CLASSIC CROCKPOT RECIPES

Courtney's Pumpkin Muesli
*Courtney Stultz
Weir, KS*

I love using the crockpot for busy days. With this recipe, I can use it for breakfast! It takes our favorite comforting breakfast, adds pumpkin and does all the work for us.

1 c. muesli cereal or steel-cut
    oats, uncooked
1 c. canned pumpkin
2 c. milk
1/2 c. brown sugar, packed,
    or coconut sugar

1 T. cinnamon
1/8 t. ground cloves
1/8 t. salt
Optional: pure maple syrup

In a lightly greased 1-1/2 quart round casserole dish, combine all ingredients except optional syrup. Stir until combined. Set dish inside a 4-quart crockpot. Pour water into crock around dish, to about one inch from top of dish. Cover and cook on low setting for 7 to 8 hours. Carefully remove dish from crockpot and stir. Serve topped with a drizzle of maple syrup, if desired. Makes 6 servings.

Honey Granola
*Barb Bargdill
Gooseberry Patch*

Great for quick breakfasts and snacking! Sometimes I'll add a handful of chocolate chips for the kids.

5 c. old-fashioned oats,
    uncooked
1-1/2 c. flaked coconut
1 c. chopped walnuts or pecans
2 T. cinnamon

3/4 c. butter, melted
3/4 c. honey
2 T. vanilla extract
1 to 2 c. dried fruit, chopped

In a 5-quart crockpot, combine oats, coconut, nuts and cinnamon; mix well. Add remaining ingredients except fruit; mix thoroughly. Partially cover and cook on low setting for 2 to 4 hours. Stir once every hour, if possible. Spread on wax paper to cool; mix in fruit. Transfer to an airtight container; keep refrigerated up to 2 weeks. Makes 8 servings.

HOT & TASTY BREAKFASTS

Cinnamon Applesauce

Becky Hahn
Manteca, CA

This is the yummiest applesauce I've ever made! I love that it is cooked in the crockpot...it makes the house smell warm and cozy like a perfect autumn day. To prep all those apples, I use an apple peeler, corer and slicer gadget I found that works amazingly well. Top with chopped pecans, walnut or granola for extra crunch.

24 Granny Smith apples, peeled,   1 T. cinnamon
   cored and sliced   1-1/2 t. vanilla extract
1 c. brown sugar, packed   1 c. water

Combine all ingredients in a 6-quart crockpot. Cover and cook on high setting for 3 to 4 hours. Turn to low setting; continue cooking until apples are fork-tender, checking occasionally. Mash with a potato masher or spoon to desired chunky or smooth consistency. For a really smooth consistency, use an immersion blender right in the crock. Let cool; cover and keep refrigerated. Makes 10 to 15 servings.

A trip to the apple orchard will give you bushels of crisp, crunchy apples to share. Spoon homemade applesauce into a Mason jar topped with a circle of homespun. Tie a raffia bow around the top...friends will love it!

Orange Sweet Rolls

JoAnn
Gooseberry Patch

Irresistible! Add a sprinkle of extra orange zest, if you like.

3 T. butter, melted
1/2 c. brown sugar, packed
  and divided
8-oz. tube refrigerated
  crescent rolls

5 T. butter, softened
1/3 c. orange marmalade

In a 4-quart crockpot, stir together melted butter and 1/4 cup brown sugar; set aside. Unroll crescent rolls and pinch seams together. Spread rolls evenly with softened butter. Spread orange marmalade over butter; sprinkle with remaining brown sugar. Roll dough tightly into a log; cut into 8 equal slices and arrange in crockpot, cut-side up. Cover and cook on high setting for one to 2 hours, until rolls are golden on the bottom. Drizzle with Orange Glaze; serve warm. Makes 8 rolls.

Orange Glaze:

1 c. powdered sugar
1 T. butter, melted

zest and juice of 1 orange

In a small bowl, combine powdered sugar, melted butter and orange zest. Add just enough orange juice to make a glaze. Stir with a fork until smooth. If glaze is too thin, add a little more powdered sugar.

Dress up the brunch table with a big bouquet of fresh-cut flowers. Keep flowers fresh a few days longer by adding a sugar cube and a spoonful of bleach to the water in the vase.

Potato Puff Breakfast Casserole

Erin Brock
Charleston, WV

This is a favorite at family brunch get-togethers...just add some sweet rolls and hot coffee!

1 lb. ground pork sausage	1/2 t. garlic powder
32-oz. pkg. frozen potato puffs, divided	1/4 t. salt
	1/8 t. pepper
6 eggs, beaten	1 c. shredded Cheddar cheese
2 T. half-and-half	Optional: chopped green onions
1/2 t. dried thyme	

Brown sausage in a skillet over medium heat, breaking up sausage as it cooks; drain. Meanwhile, add 2/3 of frozen potato puffs to a greased 5-quart crockpot; set aside. In a large bowl, whisk together eggs, half-and-half and seasonings; pour over potato puffs in crock. Layer with browned sausage, remaining potato puffs and cheese. Cover and cook on high setting for 2 to 3 hours, or on low setting for 4 to 6 hours. Garnish portions with green onions, if desired. Serves 8.

If a recipe calls for adding a spritz of non-stick vegetable spray to the crock, try using a disposable plastic crockpot liner instead. Clean-up will be a breeze!

CLASSIC CROCKPOT RECIPES

Cinnamon French Toast Casserole

*Roberta Simpkins
Mentor on the Lake, OH*

*This recipe was given to me by a co-worker and has become
a favorite, especially when we have breakfast for dinner!
It's delicious with a drizzle of fresh maple syrup.*

2 loaves sliced cinnamon swirl
    bread, cut into 1/2-inch cubes
1 doz. eggs, beaten
4 c. 2% milk
1/4 c. brown sugar, packed

2 t. vanilla extract
2 t. cinnamon
1/2 t. salt
Garnish: powdered sugar, pure
    maple syrup, fresh berries

The day before, spread bread cubes on a baking sheet to dry. Coat a
6-quart crockpot with non-stick vegetable spray; add bread cubes to
crockpot. In a bowl, whisk together remaining ingredients except
garnish; spoon over bread cubes. Cover and cook on low setting for
6 hours, removing lid for the last 30 minutes of cooktime. Spoon into
bowls; serve topped with powdered sugar, maple syrup and berries.
Makes 6 to 8 servings.

No-fuss breakfast sausages for a crowd...easier than in a skillet.
Arrange cook & serve sausage links in a rimmed baking pan
so the links aren't quite touching. Bake at 350 degrees for
12 to 15 minutes, turning halfway through. For a more
golden look, broil for the last 3 minutes.

Maple-Brown Sugar Oatmeal

Annette Ingram
Grand Rapids, MI

A favorite in fall and winter! Steel-cut oats are perfect for overnight oatmeal...they won't turn mushy during slow cooking.

softened butter or canola oil
   as needed
2 c. steel-cut oats, uncooked
4 c. water
3 c. milk
1/4 c. brown sugar, packed

1/4 c. pure maple syrup
2 t. cinnamon
1 t. vanilla extract
1/4 t. salt
Garnish: additional milk,
   brown sugar

Grease a 5-quart crockpot with butter or canola oil. Add remaining ingredients except garnish; stir well. Cover and cook on low setting for 6 to 8 hours, or on high setting for 3 to 4 hours. At serving time, top with additional milk and brown sugar, as desired. Makes 8 servings.

Early birds will appreciate finding a crockpot of overnight oatmeal awaiting them in the morning! Set out brown sugar and other yummy toppings, so everyone can fix their own.

CLASSIC CROCKPOT RECIPES

Garden-Fresh Omelet

Vickie
Gooseberry Patch

*An easy brunch recipe! Feel free to use your favorite veggies,
and add some chopped ham or crispy bacon, if you like.*

1 c. broccoli flowerets, finely
  chopped
1/2 c. red pepper, diced
1/2 c. yellow onion, finely
  chopped
2 cloves garlic, minced
8 eggs, beaten
1/2 c. milk

1/4 c. grated Parmesan cheese
1-1/2 t. Italian seasoning
1/2 t. garlic powder
salt and pepper to taste
1 c. shredded Cheddar cheese
Optional: snipped fresh parsley,
  diced ripe tomatoes

Lightly grease a 6-quart crockpot. Add broccoli, red pepper, onion and
garlic; set aside. In a large bowl, whisk together eggs, milk, Parmesan
cheese and seasonings until well blended. Pour egg mixture over
vegetables in crock. Cover and cook on high setting for 1-1/2 to 2 hours,
or on low setting for 3 to 3-1/2 hours, until eggs are set. Sprinkle with
cheese; cover and let stand for a few minutes, until cheese is melted. Cut
into wedges; lift out using a pancake turner. Garnish as desired and
serve. Serves 6 to 8.

For a light, refreshing brunch beverage, combine equal parts
chilled pomegranate juice, orange juice and sparkling water.
Pour into stemmed glasses and serve.

Strawberry Patch Jam

Claire Bertram
Lexington, KY

When strawberry season arrives in late spring, my kids and I love to go to the pick-your-own farm. We fill our pails (taste testing a few, of course!) and bring the ripe berries home to make jam. Then we enjoy our homemade jam on breakfast toast all summer long.

1-1/2 qts. ripe strawberries, hulled
5 c. sugar
1/3 c. lemon juice
9 1/2-pt. plastic freezer containers with lids, sterilized

Add strawberries to a 4-quart crockpot; stir in sugar and lemon juice. Cover and cook on high setting for 2-1/2 hours, stirring twice. Remove lid; continue cooking 2 hours longer, or until thickened, stirring occasionally. Ladle jam into sterilized freezer containers; add lids. Keep refrigerated up to 2 weeks, or freeze up to 2 months. Thaw frozen jam overnight in the refrigerator before using. Makes 9, 1/2-pint containers.

Give a "Special Delivery" breakfast to someone under the weather. Fill a basket with homemade jam and several fresh-baked muffins. Tie a ribbon around the handle, then visit a favorite friend. Sure to be appreciated!

CLASSIC CROCKPOT RECIPES

South-of-the-Border Breakfast Casserole

Debra Johnson
Myrtle Beach, SC

Friends expect this recipe to be on the menu for our tailgating brunches. Our kids love leftovers wrapped up in a tortilla for breakfast burritos. You can't go wrong with this recipe!

1 lb. ground pork sausage
1-oz. pkg. taco seasoning mix
1/3 c. water
8 eggs, beaten
1 c. half-and-half
3 c. shredded Mexican-blend
   cheese

5 c. frozen shredded
   hashbrowns, thawed
4-oz. can diced green chiles
8-oz. pkg. cream cheese, cubed
Optional: chopped ripe tomatoes,
   sliced green onions, sour
   cream, salsa

Brown sausage in a skillet over medium heat; drain. Stir in taco seasoning mix and water. Simmer over medium heat for one minute, stirring constantly. In a large bowl, whisk together eggs and half-and-half. Stir in cheese, hashbrowns, chiles and browned sausage. Carefully stir in cream cheese; transfer mixture to a greased 5-quart crockpot. Cover crock with a paper towel to absorb condensation. Cover and cook on high setting for 3 to 3-1/2 hours, turning crock after 1-1/2 hours, until set. Garnish as desired. Makes 6 to 8 servings.

A cool fruit salad goes well with hot brunch dishes. Combine blueberries, strawberries, kiwi fruit and pineapple cubes. Toss with poppy seed dressing; sprinkle with chopped fresh mint and chill.

HOT & TASTY BREAKFASTS

Biscuits & Gravy Bake

Emma Brown
Saskatchewan, Canada

Hot, hearty and so easy!

1 lb. ground pork breakfast
    sausage
8 eggs
1-1/2 c. shredded Cheddar
    cheese

salt and pepper to taste
8-oz. tube refrigerated buttermilk
    biscuits
2 14-oz. cans sausage gravy

Brown sausage in a skillet; drain and set aside. Beat eggs in a large bowl; fold in browned sausage and cheese. Season generously with salt and pepper. Pour mixture into a greased 4-quart crockpot. Cut each biscuit into 6 pieces; arrange evenly on top. Cover and cook on high setting for 2 hours, or on low setting for 4 hours, until eggs are set and biscuits are cooked through. Heat gravy in a saucepan over medium heat. To serve, divide egg mixture among plates; top with hot gravy. Serves 8 to 10.

Mountain Man Breakfast

Geneva Rogers,
Gillette, WY

Our favorite breakfast when we go RV camping!
Really sets you up for a day of hiking fun.

32-oz. pkg. frozen diced potatoes
1 lb. cooked ham, diced, or
    bacon, crisply cooked
    and crumbled
1/2 onion, chopped
1 green pepper, chopped

salt and pepper to taste
1-1/2 c. shredded Cheddar
    cheese
1 doz. eggs, beaten
3/4 c. evaporated milk

In a greased 6-quart crockpot, layer 1/3 each of frozen potatoes, ham or bacon, onion and green pepper. Season with salt and pepper; layer with 1/3 of cheese. Repeat layering twice. Beat eggs in a large bowl; whisk in milk and pour over layers in crock. Cover and cook on low setting for 6 to 8 hours. Serves 8 to 10.

CLASSIC CROCKPOT RECIPES

Babchi's Hot Chocolate

Paula Marchesi
Auburn, PA

Nothing tastes better on a snowy winter day (or night!) than a mug of this hot chocolate. It's smooth, creamy and delicious.

6 c. whole milk
2 c. whipping cream
1/2 c. sugar
8-oz. pkg. semi-sweet baking
chocolate, coarsely chopped
1/4 c. Dutch process baking
cocoa

2 t. vanilla extract
Garnish: whipped cream,
chocolate shavings, candy
sprinkles, mini marshmallows

Combine all ingredients except garnish in a 4-quart crockpot. Whisk vigorously for one to 2 minutes, until cocoa is well mixed. Cover and cook on low setting for 6 hours, or on high setting for 4 hours, stirring well every 45 minutes or so. Serve hot in mugs, garnished as desired. Makes 8 to 10 servings.

Keep the week's menus and shopping list right at your fingertips. Criss-cross a bulletin board with wide rick-rack and just slip lists underneath...so handy!

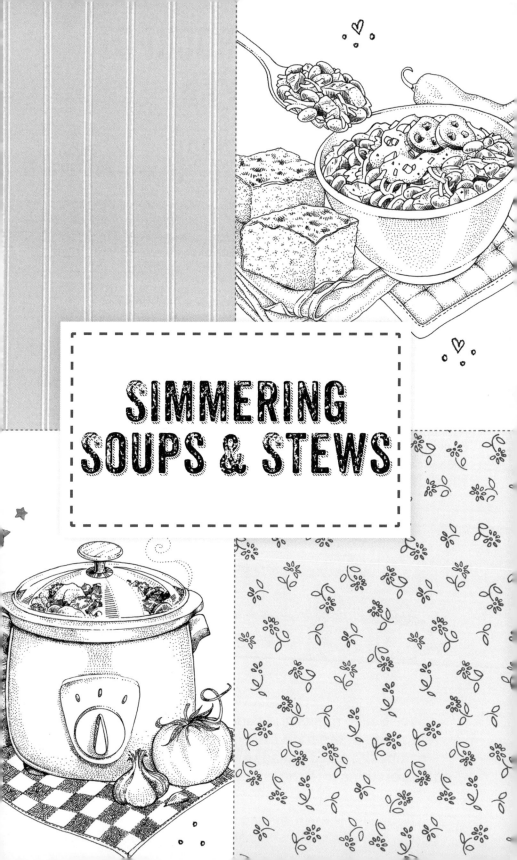

SIMMERING SOUPS & STEWS

CLASSIC CROCKPOT RECIPES

Wendy's Vegetable Soup

Wendy Vura
McKinney, TX

I started making this soup when my kids were little, as we know children don't always want to eat their vegetables. They would gobble it up, and that made this momma happy! Ground beef can be used, browning it first...cook for 6 hours total. For some zing, use Mexican tomatoes with green chiles instead of regular tomatoes.

1 lb. beef round steak, cubed
14-1/2 oz. can diced tomatoes
2 c. potatoes, peeled and cubed
3/4 c. onion, diced
2 stalks celery, sliced
2 carrots, peeled and sliced

3 cubes beef bouillon
3 c. water
1/2 t. dried oregano
1/2 t. salt
1/4 t. pepper
1-1/2 c. frozen mixed vegetables

In a 6-quart crockpot, combine beef cubes, tomatoes with juice and remaining ingredients except frozen vegetables. Mix gently. Cover and cook on high setting for 6 hours. Stir in frozen vegetables. Cover and cook on high setting for 2 more hours, or until beef and vegetables are tender. Makes 8 servings.

Slice & dice meats and veggies the night before and refrigerate in separate plastic zipping bags. Cubed meat can be browned ahead of time, too. In the morning, toss everything into the crockpot and you're on your way.

Lemon-Orzo Chicken Soup

Stephanie D'Esposito
Ravena, NY

I make this yummy soup on snowy days...it's the perfect comfort food!

6 c. chicken broth
3 T. chicken soup base
1 onion, chopped
2 stalks celery with leaves, chopped
1 large carrot, peeled and chopped
3 cloves garlic, chopped

2 boneless, skinless chicken breasts
garlic powder, onion powder, Italian seasoning or pepper to taste
1 lemon, halved
1/2 c. orzo pasta, uncooked

In a large saucepan, bring chicken broth to a boil over high heat. Add soup base; stir until dissolved. Pour broth into a 4-quart crockpot; add vegetables. Sprinkle chicken breasts with desired seasoning; arrange on top of vegetables. Squeeze lemon halves into crock; add lemon halves to crock. Cover and cook on high setting for 3 to 4 hours, or on low setting for 7 to 8 hours, until chicken is very tender. Discard lemon halves. Remove chicken and shred; return to crock. Stir in pasta; cover and cook on high setting for 30 minutes. Makes 6 servings.

Be sure to use the right-size crockpot...they work best when filled 1/2 to 2/3 full.

CLASSIC CROCKPOT RECIPES

Pork & Bean Soup

Lynda Robson
Boston, MA

Down-home hearty and so simple to make! I use my food processor
to chop all the veggies. Add some warm cornbread and serve.

1-1/4 c. dried mixed beans,
   rinsed and sorted
1 lb. pork loin, cut into
   1-inch cubes
3 T. canola oil
15-oz. can low-sodium
   chicken broth
2 c. water

3/4 c. onion, diced
1/2 c. green pepper, diced
1/2 c. baby carrots, sliced
1/2 c. celery, chopped
3 cloves garlic, minced
1/2 t. dried oregano
1/2 t. dried thyme
1 t. seasoned salt

In a large bowl, cover beans with water; soak overnight. In the morning,
drain beans; add to a 5-quart crockpot and set aside. Brown pork cubes
in oil in a skillet over medium heat; drain. Add browned pork and
remaining ingredients to crockpot; stir gently. Cover and cook on low
setting for 7 to 8 hours, until pork is very tender. Stir again and serve.
Makes 6 servings.

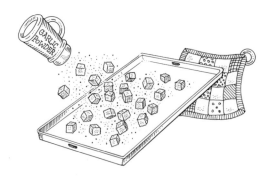

Top your favorite soup with crunchy garlic croutons.
Thinly slice a French baguette. Dip baguette slices into
a mixture of 1/2 cup melted butter and 1/2 teaspoon garlic
powder. Place on a baking sheet and broil for about
5 minutes, until crisp and golden.

Sandy's Chili Soup

*Sandy Paulin
Bloomington, IN*

*A favorite of our family during the cold winter months.
We like to enjoy it with crackers and cheese.*

1 lb. lean ground beef
1/2 c. onion, diced
2 c. elbow macaroni, uncooked
64-oz. bottle tomato juice
5-1/2 oz. can spicy cocktail
    vegetable juice

15-1/2 oz. can chili beans
14-1/2 oz. can whole tomatoes,
    quartered
5 to 6 T. chili powder, to taste

In a skillet over medium heat, brown beef with onion until no longer
pink; drain. Meanwhile, cook macaroni according to package directions;
drain. In a 5-quart crockpot, combine beef mixture, cooked macaroni
and remaining ingredients. Stir gently. Cover and cook on low setting
for 4 to 5 hours. Serves 8 to 10.

Diane's White Chili

*Diane Hixon
Niceville, FL*

I love crockpots and 5 ingredients & under recipes.

48-oz. jar Great Northern beans
2 lbs. cooked chicken, cubed
16-oz. jar favorite salsa

8-oz. pkg. Monterey Jack cheese
    with jalapeño peppers, cubed
2 t. ground cumin

In a 6-quart crockpot, combine undrained beans and remaining
ingredients. Stir to mix. Cover and cook on high setting for one hour.
Turn to low setting; cook another 2 to 3 hours. Stir again and serve.
Makes 6 servings.

There's no such thing as too much
chili! Top hot dogs and baked potatoes
with extra chili...spoon into flour
tortillas and sprinkle with shredded
cheese for quick burritos.

Farmstand Corn Chowder

Alicia Soncksen
Lincoln, NE

Every summer, we go to our local farmers' market and buy fresh sweet corn. Then we spend the afternoon cooking and freezing it so we can enjoy fresh sweet corn all through winter! This is one of our favorite winter chowders, because the fresh corn adds so much flavor.

6 ears sweet corn, kernels cut
    off, or 4-1/2 c. frozen corn
4 to 5 russet potatoes, peeled
    and diced
1/2 c. sweet onion, diced
32-oz. container chicken broth
2-1/2 c. milk
14-oz. pkg. Kielbasa sausage,
    diced
12-oz. pkg. pasteurized
    American cheese, cubed

14-3/4 oz. can cream-style corn
10-3/4 oz. can cream of
    chicken soup
10-3/4 oz. can cream of
    mushroom soup
salt and pepper to taste
Optional: 1 T. cornstarch,
    1 T. water

Combine all except optional ingredients in a 6-quart crockpot; stir well. Cover and cook on low setting for 6 to 8 hours, or on high setting for 3 to 4 hours. If consistency is too thin when done, combine cornstarch and water; stir into chowder and cook until thickened to desired consistency. Repeat, if necessary. Makes 8 servings.

Soup is the song of the hearth...and the home.
– Louis P. De Gouy

SIMMERING SOUPS & STEWS

Favorite Split Pea Soup

Wendy Vura
McKinney, TX

I had never tasted split pea soup until a friend invited me over for lunch on a cold winter's day. I modified her recipe, making it an easy crockpot meal. I have made many people split pea believers. Even children who don't think they like split pea soup will eat this and ask for more! Sometimes if I have a leftover ham bone, I will substitute ham & bone for Italian sausage, removing the bone before serving. It's wonderful both ways!

1 lb. ground Italian pork sausage
2 c. dried split peas, rinsed
    and sorted
4 c. chicken broth
4 c. water
2 onions, chopped

2 carrots, peeled and cubed
2 stalks celery, cubed
2 cubes chicken bouillon
1/4 t. garlic salt
1 t. salt
1/2 t. pepper

Brown sausage in a skillet over medium heat; drain. Combine sausage and remaining ingredients in a 6-quart crockpot; stir gently. Cover and cook on low setting for 8 to 9 hours. Makes 8 servings.

Do you have a favorite soup recipe you'd like to make in your crockpot? A recipe that simmers for one to 2 hours on the stovetop can cook on the low setting for 6 to 8 hours without overcooking.

Beef Barley Soup

Tammy Navarro
Littleton, CO

Living in Colorado, we get some pretty cold winter nights.
Served with a slice of my homemade bread, this hearty soup
is very comforting.

2 T. bacon drippings or oil
3 lbs. stew beef cubes
14-1/2 oz. can diced tomatoes
6 c. beef broth
2 carrots, peeled and thinly sliced
2 stalks celery, chopped
1/2 c. onion, diced
4 cloves garlic, minced

1 T. fresh parsley, chopped
1 t. dried oregano
1/2 t. dried thyme
1 c. pearled barley, uncooked
1 bay leaf
Optional: salt and pepper to taste
14-1/2 oz. can corn, drained

Heat drippings or oil in a large skillet over medium-high heat. Add beef cubes and cook until browned on all sides; drain. Add beef to a 6-quart crockpot. Add tomatoes with juice and remaining ingredients except corn; stir well. Cover and cook on low setting for 6 to 8 hours. Stir in corn during last 30 minutes of cooking. Discard bay leaf and serve. Makes 10 servings.

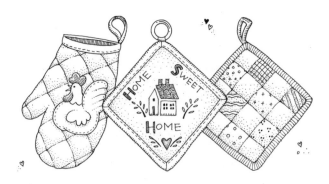

Browning adds delicious color and flavor to slow-cooked meats. Toss beef or pork cubes with flour and brown in a skillet with a little oil. If you're pressed for time, this step can be skipped. Ground meat is the exception... browning eliminates excess grease.

SIMMERING SOUPS & STEWS

After-Church Beef Stew

Mark Rushlow
Westland, MI

My mom often served this stew for dinner after Sunday noon Mass, and then later in the day we would have a lighter meal.

2 lbs. stew beef cubes
10 russet potatoes, peeled
  and cubed
1/2 red onion, finely chopped
1 c. celery, chopped

16-oz. pkg. frozen peas
16-oz. pkg. frozen sliced carrots
19-oz. can tomato-basil soup
salt and pepper to taste

Combine all ingredients in a 6-quart crockpot. Cover and cook on high setting for 2 hours. Turn to low setting; continue cooking for 4 hours. Serves 8 to 10.

Vintage tea towels are perfect for lining bread baskets. They'll keep freshly baked rolls toasty warm and add a dash of color to the table.

CLASSIC CROCKPOT RECIPES

Turkey Chili

Sharon Nunn
Mechanicsville, VA

This is my favorite chili recipe. It's full of veggies and very satisfying. Add your favorite chili toppings...I like cheese and sour cream. Leftovers are great on a baked potato!

1 lb. lean ground turkey
1 c. onion, chopped
3/4 c. green pepper, chopped
3 cloves garlic, minced
14-1/2 oz. can low-sodium
   chicken broth
28-oz. can no-salt-added diced
   tomatoes, undrained
6-oz. can tomato paste
15-1/4 oz. can corn, drained

15-oz. can kidney beans,
   drained and rinsed
15-oz. can black beans, drained
   and rinsed
1 T. chili powder
1/2 t. ground cumin
1/2 t. salt
1/4 t. pepper
Garnish: favorite chili toppings

In a large skillet over medium heat, brown turkey with onion, green pepper and garlic. Drain; transfer to a 4-quart crockpot. Add chicken broth, tomatoes with juice, tomato paste, corn, all beans and seasonings; stir to combine well. Cover and cook on low setting for 4 to 5 hours. Stir again; serve with favorite toppings. Serves 6.

Here's a fun new way to serve cornbread...waffle-style!
Mix up the batter, thin it slightly with a little extra milk and
bake in a waffle iron until crisp. Terrific for dunking!

SIMMERING SOUPS & STEWS

Idaho Potato Chowder

Norma Burton
Kuna, ID

My husband's roots go down deep in Idaho. He loves his potatoes and this comforting potato chowder! Top with sliced green onions and crisp crumbled bacon for added flavor.

32-oz. pkg. frozen diced
   potatoes, thawed
1 c. milk
1/4 c. all-purpose flour
1 t. salt
1/2 t. pepper

32-oz. container chicken broth
12-oz. pkg. frozen chopped
   broccoli, thawed
3 c. shredded Cheddar cheese
Optional: sliced green onions,
   cooked and crumbled bacon

Add potatoes to a 6-quart crockpot; set aside. In a large bowl, whisk together milk, flour, salt and pepper; stir in chicken broth. Pour over potatoes in crockpot and mix together. Cover and cook on low setting for 6 to 8 hours, until potatoes are tender. Stir in broccoli and cheese. Cook an additional 10 minutes, or until broccoli is cooked to desired tenderness and cheese is melted. Stir well. Garnish with onions and bacon, if desired. Makes 6 to 8 servings.

Bouillon cubes are a great substitute for canned broth... they save space in the pantry too. When using bouillon in soups, you may wish to adjust the amount of salt added.

Stuffed Pepper Soup

Amber Messenger
Marshallville, OH

I love serving this delicious soup spooned over homemade mashed potatoes. Along with my meatloaf, it's one of my fiance's favorite meals that I make.

1 lb. ground beef
1 onion, chopped
1 t. dried oregano
1 t. garlic salt
1 t. pepper
3 green and/or red
    peppers, chopped

2 14-1/2 oz. cans diced tomatoes
15-oz. can tomato sauce
1 c. water
1 T. Worcestershire sauce
1 c. long-cooking rice,
    uncooked

Brown beef with onion in a skillet over medium heat; drain. Stir in seasonings; transfer to a 4-quart crockpot. Add peppers, tomatoes with juice, tomato sauce, water and Worcestershire sauce. Cook rice according to package instructions; add to crockpot. Cover and cook on low setting for 6 to 8 hours. Makes 5 servings.

Add zest to a soup recipe, at no extra effort or cost.
Just choose a seasoned variety of canned diced tomatoes
like Italian or Mexican.

SIMMERING SOUPS & STEWS

Taco Vegetable Soup

Jan Mullannix
Georgetown, KY

Very good and easy. If you want it spicier,
add a little hot pepper sauce.

1 lb. ground beef or ground
    turkey breast
1/2 c. onion, chopped
2 16-oz. pkgs. frozen mixed
    vegetables

5 c. chicken broth
16-oz. jar mild or spicy salsa
1-oz. pkg. taco seasoning mix
Optional: crushed tortilla chips

In a skillet over medium heat, brown beef or turkey with onion; drain. Transfer to a 6-quart crockpot; add remaining ingredients except garnish. Mix well. Cover and cook on low setting for 7 to 8 hours. If desired, sprinkle servings with crushed tortilla chips. Serves 10 to 12.

Crista's Best Chili

Crista Stonebraker
Columbus, OH

This is a great recipe to toss together in the morning for
a yummy supper in the evening! Serve with cornbread.

1-1/2 lbs. stew beef cubes
14-1/2 oz. can diced tomatoes
    with green chiles
5 15-1/2 oz. cans assorted
    chili beans

15-1/2 oz. can black beans,
    drained
11-oz. can sweet corn & diced
    peppers, drained

Add beef cubes to a 6-quart crockpot; pour tomatoes with juice on top. Add all beans and corn; stir to combine. Cover and cook on low setting for 7 to 8 hours, until beef is very tender. Makes 8 servings.

Cut soup vegetables into equal-size
pieces for even cooking.

CLASSIC CROCKPOT RECIPES

Hearty Fish Chowder

Audrey Lett
Newark, DE

*This tasty chowder can be made with codfish, haddock or flounder...
really, any mild white fish. Serve with saltines.*

1 lb. white fish fillets, thawed if
    frozen, cut into large chunks
2 cloves garlic, minced
3/4 c. onion, chopped
2 potatoes, peeled and diced
2 carrots, peeled and sliced
1 stalk celery, sliced
1 c. fresh or frozen corn
4 c. fish or seafood broth
1 t. dried thyme
salt and pepper to taste
1 c. whole milk

In a 5-quart crockpot, combine fish fillets, garlic and vegetables. Add broth and thyme; season with salt and pepper. Mix gently. Cover and cook on low setting for 4 hours, or until fish is cooked through and vegetables are tender. Stir in milk and cook for an additional 10 minutes. Makes 4 servings.

Vintage coffee mugs are fun for serving soup...
warm your hands on chilly days, too. Pick up
one-of-a-kind novelty or souvenir mugs cheaply
at thrift stores and yard sales.

New England Clam Chowder *Irene Robinson*
Cincinnati, OH

A yummy, low-fat soup that's a snap to put together...perfect on chilly days. Please pass the oyster crackers!

2 to 3 6-1/2 oz. cans chopped
  clams
2 10-3/4 oz. cans low-fat
  cream of celery soup
10-3/4 oz. can low-fat cream of
  mushroom soup

16-oz. pkg. frozen diced potatoes
2 c. non-fat half-and-half
2 T. real bacon bits
1/4 t. pepper

Combine undrained clams and remaining ingredients in a lightly greased 4-quart crockpot; mix well. Cover and cook on low setting for 4 to 5 hours. Stir again and serve. Makes 8 servings.

Chowder is extra hearty served in bread bowls. Cut the tops off round crusty loaves and scoop out the soft bread inside. Brush with olive oil and bake at 350 degrees for a few minutes, until toasty. Fill and serve.

CLASSIC CROCKPOT RECIPES

Creamy Chicken Noodle Soup

Becky Shanahan
Strasburg, PA

I love this recipe because you can substitute different vegetables, types of pasta and seasonings, and it still turns out amazing each time! It's hard to get bored when you can change it up each time. I start making this soup when the weather gets brisk and it keeps me warm until spring arrives. This soup will serve the whole family and is perfect after a cold day spent outdoors, sledding or building a snowman.

4 boneless, skinless chicken
    thighs
2 to 4 T. Tuscan herb seasoning
    or other favorite savory
    spice mix
2 c. celery, chopped
2 c. carrots, peeled and chopped

2 c. onion, chopped
2 c. chicken broth or water
8-oz. pkg. gemelli, orzo or other
    small pasta, uncooked
1 c. whipping cream
salt and pepper to taste

Sprinkle chicken thighs with herb seasoning to taste. Layer chicken in a 6-quart crockpot. Cover and cook on high setting for 4 hours, or until chicken is tender. Remove chicken to a plate; shred or chop and return to crock. Add vegetables and chicken broth or water. Cover and continue cooking on high setting for another 30 minutes, or until vegetables are tender. Add pasta; cover and cook on high setting for another 20 minutes. Turn off crockpot; stir in cream. Add additional broth or water if needed; season with salt and pepper to taste. Makes 6 to 8 servings.

For the freshest flavor, add an extra pinch of herbs at the end of cooking time. Dried herbs tend to lose their flavor during long simmering.

SIMMERING SOUPS & STEWS

Kitchen Pantry Soup

Alice Joy Randall
Nacogdoches, TX

One day I wanted soup, but something different, and came up with this recipe from the ingredients I had on hand. If you own a can opener, you can make this! Serve with cornbread.

12-1/2 oz. can chunk
  chicken breast
15-1/2 oz. can Great
  Northern beans
14-1/2 oz. can diced tomatoes
  & green chiles

14-3/4 oz. can corn
10-3/4 oz. can cream of
  chicken soup
Optional: 2 c. cabbage, chopped
salt and pepper to taste

Add chicken to a 4-quart crockpot; shred any large chunks with a fork. Add remaining ingredients; do not drain cans. Stir well. Cover and cook on high setting for 4 hours, or to desired consistency. Makes 6 servings.

Crunchy cheese toasts...yum! Brush thin slices of French bread lightly with olive oil. Broil for 2 to 3 minutes, until golden. Turn over; sprinkle with shredded Parmesan cheese and Italian seasoning. Broil another 2 to 3 minutes, until cheese melts...place on bowls of hot soup. Yum!

CLASSIC CROCKPOT RECIPES

Gigi's Chicken & Tortellini Soup

Becky Norager Bosen
Layton, UT

This is an easy yet hearty and delicious soup to toss together on a crisp fall or winter day. A real "stick-to-your-ribs" meal! Serve with crusty bread, hot biscuits or saltine crackers.

2 boneless, skinless
   chicken breasts
6 c. chicken broth
3/4 c. onion, diced
1 carrot, peeled and sliced
2 t. dried rosemary
2 t. dried tarragon
2 t. dried thyme
3/4 t. garlic powder
1 t. salt
1/2 t. pepper
1 c. whipping cream
19-oz. pkg. frozen cheese
   tortellini pasta, uncooked

In a 5-quart crockpot, combine all ingredients except cream and tortellini. Cover and cook on low setting for 6 hours, or until chicken is tender. Remove chicken and shred; return chicken to crock. Add cream and tortellini; stir. Cover and cook on low setting for another 45 to 50 minutes, until tortellini is tender but not overcooked. Makes 6 servings.

Keep a container in the freezer for leftover veggies, then make a big pot of vegetable soup. Thaw and add to a crockpot. Add a can of tomato sauce or broth, seasonings and enough water to fill crock 2/3 full. Cover and cook on low all day...delicious!

SIMMERING SOUPS & STEWS

Chicken & Vegetable Soup

Angela Bissette
Wilson, NC

This is a recipe I came up with when I wanted a hearty one-dish dinner. Serve with fresh bread for a complete meal.

4 potatoes, peeled and cubed
2 c. frozen green beans
2 carrots, peeled and sliced
3/4 c. onion, cubed
6 boneless, skinless
    chicken thighs

10-3/4 oz. can golden
    mushroom soup
1 c. chicken broth

Layer all vegetables in a 6-quart crockpot; place chicken thighs on top. Whisk together mushroom soup and chicken broth in a bowl; spoon over chicken. Cover and cook on low setting for 7 to 8 hours, until chicken is very tender. Shred chicken in crock; stir into soup and serve. Makes 6 servings.

If you need your crock to begin cooking while you're away, plug it into an automatic timer. Well-chilled foods can safely be held at room temperature for one to 2 hours.

CLASSIC CROCKPOT RECIPES

Amazing Chicken Enchilada Soup

Marla Kinnersley
Surprise, AZ

This is the recipe that got me hooked on using my crockpot. It's so simple to toss everything in! Then when you come home 8 hours later, the house smells fabulous and everyone loves eating this.

1 T. butter
1 T. olive oil
1 onion, chopped
4 cloves garlic, minced
2 boneless, skinless chicken
  breasts
15-1/2 oz. can black beans,
  drained and rinsed
15-oz. can white shoepeg
  corn, drained
14-1/2 oz. can diced tomatoes
  with green chiles
10-oz. can mild red enchilada
  sauce

32-oz. container chicken broth
4 t. chicken soup base
1/2 t. dry mustard
1/2 t. onion powder
1/2 t. garlic powder
1/2 t. chili powder
1/2 t. ground cumin
1/8 t. cinnamon
8-oz. pkg. cream cheese,
  unwrapped
Garnish: sliced avocado, snipped
  fresh cilantro, tortilla strips

Melt butter with oil in a skillet over medium heat. Cook onion until golden; add garlic and cook for another minute. In a 6-quart crockpot, layer chicken breasts, onion mixture, beans, corn, tomatoes with juice, sauce, broth and seasonings. Stir well; place block of cream cheese on top. Cover and cook on low setting for 8 hours, or until chicken is very tender. Shred chicken; return to soup and stir well. Serve with desired toppings. Makes 8 servings.

Frozen leftovers from a slow-cooked meal make great quick lunches and dinners. Thaw and reheat them using the microwave, stovetop or oven...crockpots don't work well for reheating frozen foods.

Spicy Turkey Chili

Suzan Mechling
Round Rock, TX

This is a delicious chili on a cold day. Great for freezing, too.

1 T. olive oil
1/2 c. onion, diced
1 stalk celery, diced
1/2 c. green pepper, diced
1-1/4 lbs. lean ground turkey
2 cloves garlic, minced
1 c. mushrooms, diced
2 14-1/2 oz. cans Mexican
    stewed tomatoes, chopped

28-oz. can tomato sauce
16-oz. can navy beans, drained
    and rinsed
15-1/2 oz. can pink pinto beans,
    drained and rinsed
1 T. chili powder
1 T. ground cumin

Heat olive oil in a large skillet over medium heat. Sauté onion, celery and green pepper for 5 minutes, or until slightly softened. Add turkey; continue cooking for an additional 5 minutes, or until no longer pink, breaking up turkey as it cooks. Stir in garlic; cook for another 30 seconds. Transfer turkey mixture to a 6-quart crockpot. Add mushrooms, stewed tomatoes with juice, tomato sauce, beans and seasonings. Stir gently, folding the bottom ingredients to the top. Cover and cook on low setting for 7 to 8 hours. Makes 10 servings.

Host a neighborhood chili cook-off. Invite everyone to bring crockpots filled with their own special chili...you provide yummy toppings, cornbread and a little prize for the winner!

CLASSIC CROCKPOT RECIPES

Ham & Cabbage Stew

Shirley Howie
Foxboro, MA

This is an old recipe from my mother's recipe box. She often made it for us, using the cabbages, carrots and onions from our own garden. It is especially good served with warm cornbread!

8-oz. pkg. cooked ham
   steak, cubed
4 c. cabbage, shredded
2 c. carrots, peeled and sliced
4-oz. can sliced mushrooms
2/3 c. beef broth

1/2 c. onion, diced
1 clove garlic, minced
1/4 t. caraway seed
1/4 t. pepper
1 T. cornstarch
2 T. water

In a 4-quart crockpot, combine all ingredients except cornstarch and water; do not drain mushrooms. Cover and cook on low setting for 4 to 6 hours, until vegetables are tender. In a small bowl, mix cornstarch and water until smooth. Stir into crockpot during last hour to thicken stew slightly. Makes 4 servings.

Wondering if your old crockpot still heats properly? Fill it 2/3 full of water, cover and cook on high setting for 4 hours. Check water with an instant-read thermometer...it will read 180 degrees if it works as it should.

SIMMERING SOUPS & STEWS

Summer Vegetable Stew

Kathy Grashoff
Fort Wayne, IN

So fresh-tasting...perfect after you've visited the farmers' market.

15-oz. can chickpeas, drained
   and rinsed
1 zucchini, halved and sliced
   1/2-inch thick
1 yellow squash, halved and
   sliced 1/2-inch thick
4 plum tomatoes, cut into
   1/2-inch cubes

1 c. fresh or frozen corn
1 c. vegetable broth
1/2 to 1 t. dried rosemary
Garnish: shredded Parmesan
   cheese, chopped fresh
   Italian parsley

In a 4-quart crockpot, combine all ingredients except garnish. Stir to
blend. Cover and cook on low setting for 6 to 7 hours, or on high setting
for 3 to 4 hours. Garnish servings as desired. Makes 4 to 6 servings.

Best Chicken Noodle Soup

Sandra Coffey
Cincinnati, OH

Yummy chicken noodle soup that my family loves...Gram style!

4 boneless, skinless chicken
   breasts
6 c. water
1 onion, chopped

2 stalks celery, chopped
salt and pepper to taste
12-oz. pkg frozen egg noodles,
   uncooked

Add all ingredients except noodles to a 6-quart crockpot. Cover and
cook on low setting for 6 to 8 hours, until chicken is very tender.
Remove chicken to a plate; cut into bite-size pieces and cover to keep
warm. Turn crockpot to high setting; add frozen noodles to broth in
crock. Cover and cook for 30 minutes, or until tender. Return chicken
to crock; mix gently and serve. Makes 6 servings.

Need to add a little zing to a pot of soup?
Add a splash of lemon juice or vinegar.

CLASSIC CROCKPOT RECIPES

Sweet-and-Sour Beef Stew
Kathy Courington
Canton, GA

The first time I made this, I thought maybe not...but it is surprisingly good. It's a nice change from the same old beef stew, with an added zing. Browned ground beef can be used instead of stew beef. Yum!

1 lb. stew beef cubes
2 T. oil
3 carrots, peeled and sliced
1 onion, chopped
8-oz. can tomato sauce
1/2 c. water

1/4 c. brown sugar
1/4 c. vinegar
2 T. Worcestershire sauce
salt and pepper to taste
cooked noodles or rice

In a skillet over medium heat, brown beef in oil; drain and transfer to a 4-quart crockpot. Add remaining ingredients except noodles or rice. Cover and cook on low setting for 6 to 8 hours, until beef is tender. Serve over cooked noodles or rice. Makes 4 servings.

A hearty dish like Sweet-and-Sour Beef Stew is perfect on a cool evening. Carry the crock right out to your backyard picnic table and enjoy the fresh air with your family!

SIMMERING SOUPS & STEWS

Bacon & Cheese Potato Soup
Donna Wilson
Maryville, TN

I found this recipe awhile back and tried it out. It was a hit with my family...very creamy and delicious. I thought I would share because it's perfect for a chilly day.

4 to 5 c. chicken broth
24-oz. pkg. frozen diced
   potatoes, plain or with
   onions & peppers
8-oz. pkg. cream cheese, cubed
4-oz. pkg. real bacon bits

10-3/4 oz. can cream of
   chicken soup
salt and pepper to taste
3 c. shredded Cheddar cheese,
   divided

Pour chicken broth into a 5-quart crockpot. Add frozen potatoes; top with cubed cream cheese. Add remaining ingredients except shredded cheese; mix gently. Top with 2 cups shredded cheese. Cover and cook on low setting for 4 to 6 hours. Stir again; serve with remaining cheese sprinkled on top. Makes 6 servings.

Easy does it! Scrub the crock liner gently...a nylon scrubbie is just right for removing cooked-on food particles.

47

CLASSIC CROCKPOT RECIPES

Chicken Tortilla Soup

Lisanne Miller
Wells, ME

This recipe works great for times when you have family & friends over for a fun weekend. It's delicious!

48-oz. can diced tomatoes
14-1/2 oz. can diced tomatoes
   with green chiles
8-oz. can fire-roasted diced
   tomatoes
8-oz. can diced tomatoes with
   onions
15-1/2 oz. can kidney beans or
   chili beans

2 boneless, skinless chicken
   breasts
1 t. garlic, minced
1-oz. pkg. mild taco seasoning
   mix
1-oz. ranch salad dressing mix
Garnish: tortilla chips, shredded
   Cheddar cheese, sliced
   jalapeño peppers, sour cream

For the best flavor, make soup ahead of time. Combine all ingredients except garnish in a 6-quart crockpot. Cover and cook on low setting for 6 hours. Shred chicken; return to soup and mix well. Transfer to a large soup pot; cover and refrigerate for 8 hours, or overnight. At serving time, reheat on the stovetop over medium-low heat. Serve garnished as desired. Makes 6 to 8 servings.

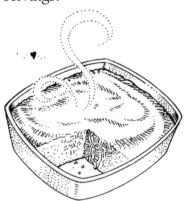

Bake up cornbread for a crowd while dinner is simmering. Combine an 8-1/2 ounce box of corn muffin mix, a 9-ounce box of yellow cake mix, 1/2 cup water, 1/3 cup milk and 2 beaten eggs. Pour into a greased 13"x9" baking pan and bake at 350 degrees for 15 to 20 minutes. Delicious!

Carolyn's Dump Soup

Carolyn Deckard
Bedford, IN

This is a good name for this soup, because that's how you put it together in a crockpot. Depends on how busy your day is!

10-3/4 oz. can Cheddar
  cheese soup
10-3/4 oz. can cream of
  broccoli soup
10-3/4 oz. can cream of
  potato soup
10-3/4 oz. can cream of
  celery soup

1-3/4 c. whole milk
3/4 c. onion, diced
2 carrots, peeled and sliced
1-1/2 T. butter, diced
celery salt, salt and pepper
  to taste

In a 5-quart crockpot, whisk together soups and milk. Add onion, carrots and butter; mix well. Cover and cook on medium setting for 2 to 3 hours, or on low setting for 3 to 4 hours. Stir in desired seasonings and serve. Makes 6 servings.

Make a bridal shower gift extra special! Fill up a new crockpot with seasoning mix packets, herbs and spices. You can even tuck in a mini cookbook...the new bride will appreciate your thoughtfulness.

CLASSIC CROCKPOT RECIPES

Cabbage & Sausage Soup

Stephanie Kemp
Lakeville, OH

This is a simple crockpot soup, perfect for a cold, winter evening. Smells so delicious to come home to after work! We love it. I often put some in the freezer to enjoy at a later time...it freezes great! This is delicious with a chewy bread to dip in the soup.

2 T. oil
1/2 c. onion, chopped
4 to 5 cloves garlic, diced
1 lb. ground beef
1 lb. ground regular or Italian
    pork sausage
14-1/2 oz. can diced tomatoes

2 t. dried oregano
2 t. dried thyme
1 t. ground cumin
1 t. red pepper flakes
4 c. beef broth
6 to 7 c. cabbage, shredded
salt and pepper to taste

Heat oil in a large skillet over medium heat; sauté onion and garlic until onion is translucent. Add beef and sausage to skillet. Cook for 4 to 5 minutes until no longer pink, breaking up with a spatula. Drain; transfer beef mixture to a lightly greased 6-quart crockpot. Add tomatoes with juice and seasonings; stir well. Add beef broth; top with cabbage. Cover and cook on high setting for 4 to 5 hours, or on low setting for 7 to 8 hours. Stir again and serve. Serves 6.

Speed up prep time on ground beef recipes! Brown several pounds of beef ahead of time, spoon into large plastic freezer bags and flatten to freeze. Thaw overnight in the fridge anytime it's needed.

TAILGATE & PARTY SANDWICHES

Garlic-Toasted BBQ Chicken Sandwiches

Alicia Soncksen
Lincoln, NE

The first time I tasted this recipe was at my aunt's house for a football party. It was so delicious that it has become a game-day favorite!

6 boneless, skinless chicken breasts
12-oz. bottle honey barbecue sauce
1/2 c. olive oil & vinegar salad dressing

1/4 c. brown sugar, packed
2 T. Worcestershire sauce
8 Italian sandwich rolls, split
small amount olive oil
garlic powder to taste

Layer chicken breasts in a 6-quart crockpot; set aside. In a large bowl, combine barbecue sauce, salad dressing, brown sugar and Worcestershire sauce; spoon over chicken. Cover and cook on low setting for 6 to 8 hours, or on high setting for 3 to 4 hours, until chicken is very tender. Remove chicken and shred with a fork; return to crock and mix with the sauce. About 30 minutes before serving time, brush cut sides of sandwich rolls with a little olive oil; sprinkle with garlic powder. Arrange rolls cut-side up on a broiler pan; toast under the broiler for 2 to 3 minutes, until golden. Serve shredded chicken in the toasted rolls. Makes 8 sandwiches.

With a crockpot, feeding a crowd is a breeze. Fill it up with your favorite shredded meat, hot dogs or meatballs. Set out bakery-fresh rolls, chips and coleslaw...and you're ready to just let guests help themselves!

TAILGATE & PARTY SANDWICHES

Italian Beef Sandwiches

Patricia Nau
River Grove, IL

This recipe is so easy in a crockpot...scrumptious, too!

4-lb. beef chuck roast
2 t. garlic, chopped
1-1/2 c. beef broth
12-oz. jar mild banana peppers,
   sliced and juice reserved

6 to 8 Italian hard rolls, split
6 to 8 slices provolone or
   mozzarella cheese

Place roast in a 6-quart crockpot. Spread garlic over roast; pour beef broth around roast. Pour peppers with reserved juice over roast. Cover and cook on low setting for 7-1/2 hours, or until roast is very tender. Uncover; shred roast with 2 forks and stir into broth. Cover and continue cooking for 30 minutes. To serve, place one big scoop of beef on the bottom half of each roll; top each with a slice of cheese. Place on a broiler pan; broil just until cheese melts. If desired, top sandwiches with some of the peppers from crockpot. Add top halves of rolls and serve. Makes 6 to 8 sandwiches.

Hot sandwich buns for a crowd...easy! Fill a roaster with buns, cover with heavy-duty aluminum foil and cut several slits in the foil. Top with several dampened paper towels and tightly cover with more foil. Bake at 250 degrees for 20 minutes, or until rolls are hot and steamy.

CLASSIC CROCKPOT RECIPES

Perfect Pulled Pork

Kimberly Redeker
Savoy, IL

When I used to live in Fort Myers, Florida, there was a restaurant that would serve slow-roasted pork on top of the best nachos ever. Since moving back to the Midwest, I have recreated the recipe so I can enjoy a taste of the tropics anytime. Hope you enjoy the depth of flavors in this dish! You can also make this recipe using the same amount of white or dark chicken and it turns out just as good.

3 to 4-lb. pork shoulder roast	10-oz. can red enchilada sauce
1 c. water	1 c. brown sugar, packed
1 onion, chopped	2 c. club soda
1/2 c. sugar	2-1/2 T. taco seasoning mix
1 t. salt	

Add pork roast to a 6-quart crockpot; top with water, onion, sugar and salt. Cover and cook on low setting for 8 hours, or until pork is very tender. For sauce, combine remaining ingredients in a saucepan; simmer over medium-low heat for 25 minutes. Shred pork; combine with sauce and serve as desired. May be made into nachos, tacos or sandwiches, or is delicious just by itself. Makes 6 to 8 servings.

Serve shredded pork in a new way...layered with lettuce and diced tomatoes in large plastic cups. Top with shredded cheese, chopped avocado and a dollop of sour cream. Provide sturdy plastic forks...guests can stroll and eat!

TAILGATE & PARTY SANDWICHES

Chicken Cheesesteaks

Danielle Boyd
Wytheville, VA

This is a great way to enjoy take-out right at home! Serve with optional toppings such as lettuce, tomato and mayonnaise.

3 boneless, skinless chicken
  breasts
20-oz. pkg. frozen pepper &
  onion blend

1 T. Montreal steak seasoning
6 sub rolls, split
12 slices provolone cheese

Place chicken breasts in a 6-quart crockpot. Top with frozen pepper & onion blend; sprinkle seasoning over all. Cover and cook on low setting for 6 hours, or on high setting for 4 hours, until chicken is very tender. Transfer chicken mixture to a large bowl; shred chicken and stir well. Divide chicken mixture among rolls; top each sandwich with 2 slices cheese and serve. Makes 6 sandwiches.

Here's a good tip for any buffet table...stack your plates at the beginning, but save the silverware, napkins and beverages for the end of the line. So much easier to handle!

CLASSIC CROCKPOT RECIPES

Hot Dog Sauce

Vivian Marshall
Columbus, OH

This is a popular tailgate recipe. It's also great for a barbecue crowd, since it makes so much. You can spoon it over hot dogs, brats or burgers in buns, or cut up hot dogs and add them right to the sauce. Either way, it's great! I have also added cooked macaroni to the leftovers to make a tasty casserole. For a different flavor, try it with 1/2 ground pork sausage (a spicy one is great!) and 1/2 ground beef.

5 lbs. lean ground beef
2 16-oz. cans sauerkraut,
   very well drained
1 c. white onion, diced
32-oz. bottle catsup
1 c. light brown sugar, packed

2 T. chili powder
15 all-beef hot dogs, cooked
15 hot dog buns, split
Optional: shredded Cheddar
   cheese

Brown beef in a large skillet over medium heat, working in batches if necessary. Drain well; transfer to a 6-quart crockpot. Add remaining ingredients except hot dogs, buns and optional cheese in order listed, mixing each one completely before adding the next to ensure a good blend. Cover and cook on high setting for 3 hours, stirring occasionally. When done, turn to low setting to keep warm until ready to use. For a thicker sauce, uncover crock after turning it to low. To serve, spoon desired amount of sauce onto hot dogs in buns; top with shredded cheese, if desired. Makes 15 servings.

Hot dogs for a crowd! Fill up a crockpot with hot dogs, standing them on end. Cover and cook on high setting for 2-1/2 to 3 hours, until the hot dogs in center of crock are heated through.

TAILGATE & PARTY SANDWICHES

French Dip Sandwiches

Andrea Gast
Lake Saint Louis, MO

So easy, but so yummy! A great weeknight meal that the whole family loves. Add a crisp salad and serve.

1 white onion, sliced
3-lb. beef chuck roast
1 t. garlic powder
10-3/4 oz. can French
   onion soup

6 to 8 slices French or Italian
   bread
6 to 8 slices provolone cheese

Spread onion slices evenly in a 5-quart crockpot. Sprinkle roast with garlic powder; add to crock on top of onion. Pour soup down the side of crock into bottom of crockpot. Cover and cook on low setting for 6 to 8 hours, until roast is very tender. Remove roast to a platter and shred. To serve, top each slice of bread with shredded beef and a cheese slice. Serve with cups of au jus from the crock on the side. Makes 6 to 8 open-face sandwiches.

Reuben Sandwiches

Pam Hooley
LaGrange, IN

I found this recipe years ago, and usually make it around Saint Patrick's Day. It's delicious and easy. Use one can of sauerkraut if you like it a little...use two if you like it a lot! I like to take the leftovers, put them between 2 pieces of rye bread, and toast them like a toasted cheese sandwich. Yummy!

12-oz. can corned beef, drained
   and flaked
1 to 2 14-1/2 oz. cans
   sauerkraut, drained
1 c. Thousand Island
   salad dressing

8-oz. pkg. Swiss cheese, cubed
   or shredded
16 slices rye bread

Combine all ingredients except bread in a 4-quart crockpot; mix gently. Cover and cook on low setting for 2 to 4 hours. Stir again; serve mixture on rye bread. Makes 8 sandwiches.

Chipped Ham Barbecue Sandwiches

Victoria McGrath
Sarver, PA

A potluck favorite in Pittsburgh and western Pennsylvania.
So easy to make...so tasty!

2 c. brown sugar, packed
2 c. catsup
3/4 c. vinegar
1/4 c. Worcestershire sauce
1 c. onion, chopped

1 clove garlic, chopped
1/2 t. pepper
1 lb. deli chipped ham
8 kaiser rolls, split, or sliced
  French bread

In a 5-quart crockpot, mix together all ingredients except ham and rolls or bread. Stir in water until mixture is the consistency of barbecue sauce. Cover and cook on high setting for 30 minutes. Turn setting to low; stir in ham. Cover and continue cooking for about 3-1/2 hours. Check sauce every 30 minutes to ensure there is enough water to keep mixture the consistency of barbecue sauce. Stir again. Serve ham mixture on kaiser rolls or French bread. Makes 8 sandwiches.

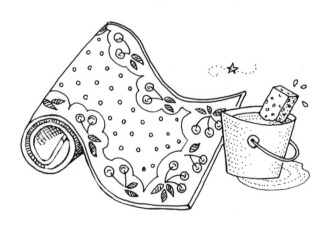

BBQ sandwiches are best served on a vintage-style oilcloth...
saucy spills wipe right up! Look for one with
a colorful design of fruit or flowers.

Chicken-Bacon Ranch Sandwiches

Maria McGovern
Stratford, NJ

I used this recipe quite a bit when I was teaching. It was great to come home to a wonderful smelling kitchen and a scrumptious dinner!

4 boneless, skinless chicken
   breasts
2 8-oz. pkgs. cream cheese,
   softened
2 c. shredded Cheddar cheese,
   divided
1-oz. pkg. ranch salad
   dressing mix

1 t. garlic powder
8 slices bacon, crisply cooked
   and crumbled
8 hoagie or sub rolls, split
   and toasted

In a 5-quart crockpot, layer chicken, cream cheese, one cup shredded cheese, ranch seasoning mix and garlic powder. Cover and cook on low setting for 7 to 8 hours, or on high setting for 3 to 4 hours. Shred chicken with 2 forks; stir into mixture in crock. Fold in crumbled bacon. Scoop chicken mixture into rolls; top with remaining cheese and serve. Makes 8 sandwiches.

Keep a big stack of bandannas on hand to use as napkins when serving juicy sandwiches.

Jamaican Jerk Pulled Pork BBQ

Pamela Matthews
Fort Thomas, KY

I first made this for my daughter's wedding. It was so well-liked that people ask me for the recipe all the time. This recipe is easily adjustable to make as much as you want. Believe me, in my household it doesn't last long! Any leftovers can be put it into plastic zipping bags to freeze for later.

1 onion, finely chopped
3 to 4-lb. pork loin
Caribbean or Jamaican jerk
   seasoning to taste
4-oz. bottle smoke-flavored
   cooking sauce, divided

2 18-oz. bottles bold & spicy
   barbecue sauce, divided
2 18-oz. bottles sweet & tangy
   barbecue sauce, divided
20 favorite buns, split, or
   sliced bread

Spread onion in a 6-quart crockpot; set aside. Rub pork loin with seasoning; add to crock. Add 1/2 bottle smoke-flavored cooking sauce and one bottle of each flavor of barbecue sauce. Cover and cook on low setting for 8 hours, or until pork is falling-apart tender. Use a meat masher to pull apart pork in crockpot. Stir in remaining smoke-flavored sauce and additional barbecue sauce to desired consistency. Taste and add more seasoning, if needed. Cover and cook on low setting for one more hour, stirring every 10 minutes or so to prevent burning. Serve pork mixture on buns or bread. Makes 20 servings or more.

Turn your favorite shredded pork and beef into party food... serve up bite-size portions on slider buns. Guests will love sampling a little of everything.

TAILGATE & PARTY SANDWICHES

Sausages with Peppers & Onions

JoAnn
Gooseberry Patch

Sausage sandwiches are a must at the local high school's annual fall festival. We wouldn't have it any other way!

3 lbs. Italian pork sausages
Optional: 1 T. oil
6 c. green and/or red peppers,
    cut into 2-inch strips
3 c. onions, sliced

2 24-oz. jars pasta sauce
8 crusty Italian rolls, split
Optional: shredded mozzarella
    cheese

Pierce sausages with a fork. If desired, brown sausages in oil in a skillet over medium heat; drain. Add sausages, peppers and onions to a 6-quart crockpot; pour pasta sauce over all. Cover and cook on low setting for 7 to 8 hours, or on high setting for 3-1/2 to 4 hours, until sausages are cooked through. Divide sausages evenly among rolls; top with sauce mixture and cheese, if desired. Makes 8 or more sandwiches.

Take along the slow crockpot on your next RV outing or camping trip. Fill the crock in the morning and dinner will practically cook itself!

Cheesy Shredded Beef Hoagies

Jesi Allen
Rock Hill, SC

Growing up in Iowa, we kids loved the smell of this recipe in the crockpot on cold days, because we knew we'd be having tasty hot sandwiches for supper. During deer season, we often used a venison roast, but beef works just as beautifully. Serve with lots of napkins. They're not neat to eat, but they are delicious!

2 to 3-lb. beef chuck roast
1-oz. pkg. onion soup mix
1 lb. sliced mushrooms
2-1/2 c. water
10-3/4 oz. can cream of
   mushroom soup
10-3/4 oz. can French
   onion soup

10-3/4 oz. can Cheddar cheese
   soup
8 hoagie rolls, split
16 slices provolone, Swiss or
   American cheese

Place roast in a 4-quart crockpot. Sprinkle with soup mix and top with mushrooms; add water. Cover and cook on low setting for 4 to 6 hours; add more water, if necessary. Remove from crockpot to a platter. Drain liquid from crockpot, reserving 3/4 to one cup broth and mushrooms; return mushrooms to crockpot. Shred roast into bite-size pieces; return beef to crock. Stir mushroom and onion soups into beef mixture along with reserved broth. Cover and cook on low setting for one hour. Stir in cheese soup; cover and cook for 30 minutes, or until heated through. Meanwhile, lightly toast hoagie rolls; place 2 slices of cheese on each roll. Place rolls under the broiler to melt cheese, if desired. Spread beef mixture generously on hoagie rolls and serve. Makes 8 sandwiches.

It's a lovely thing, everyone
sitting down together,
sharing food.

– Alice May Brock

TAILGATE & PARTY SANDWICHES

Sloppy Chicken Sandwiches

Jennifer Dorward
Winder, GA

An Ohio Amish county favorite! Use potato chips or a sleeve of buttery round crackers instead of the stuffing if you like, but if you do, be sure to add some onion and garlic powder for more flavor. Add a slice of Swiss cheese to your sammie! Mmm, mmm. If you don't want a sandwich, serve over mashed potatoes or rice.

4 boneless, skinless chicken
  breasts
2 10-3/4 oz. cans cream of
  chicken soup
6-oz. pkg. chicken-flavored
  stuffing mix
1 c. chicken broth
6 to 8 hamburger buns, split

Place chicken breasts in a 5-quart crockpot; top with chicken soup. Cover and cook on high setting for 4 hours, or until chicken is very tender. Shred chicken in crock with 2 forks. Stir in stuffing mix and chicken broth. Cover and cook another 30 minutes, or until creamy and juicy. Serve chicken mixture on hamburger buns. Makes 6 to 8 sandwiches.

Easy Pulled Pork

Annette Smith
Berryville, VA

I love this simple pork on buns, or served with coleslaw.

2 to 2-1/2 lb. pork loin
1 to 1-1/2 18-oz. bottles favorite
  barbecue sauce
1/4 c. brown sugar, packed
4 sandwich buns, split

Add pork loin to a 4-quart crockpot, cutting to fit if necessary. Add barbecue sauce and brown sugar. Cover and cook on low setting for 6 to 8 hours, until pork is very tender. Shred pork with 2 forks; stir into sauce in crock. Serve pork on buns. Makes 4 sandwiches.

For variety when serving shredded meats, slice up a French or Italian loaf into bun-size lengths.

Juicy & Tender French Dip Sandwiches

Lori Rosenberg
Cleveland, OH

My secret ingredient to make this beef so tender is...lemon-lime soda! Somehow, and I don't know why, it really makes a difference in the taste. I discovered this accidentally when I didn't have any cola in the house!

1 T. olive oil
3-lb. beef chuck roast,
    fat trimmed
1/3 c. reduced-sodium soy sauce
1 c. lemon-lime soda (not diet)
2 10-1/2 oz. cans beef
    consomme
1/4 c. dried, minced onions
1 T. beef bouillon granules
1 t. garlic powder

1/2 t. onion powder
1/2 t. dried oregano
1/4 t. dried thyme
1/2 t. salt
1/4 t. pepper
1 bay leaf
6 French rolls or hoagie
    buns, split
12 slices provolone cheese

In a large non-stick skillet, heat olive oil over medium-high heat. Using tongs or 2 forks to hold roast, lightly brown roast on all sides. Transfer roast to a 5-quart crockpot; top with remaining ingredients except buns and cheese. Cover and cook on low setting for 4 hours. Remove roast to a cutting board; thinly slice roast across the grain. Return sliced beef to liquid in crockpot; cover and continue to cook on low setting for one to 2 additional hours. At serving time, remove roast from crock; strain fat from broth for dipping. Discard bay leaf. Arrange bottoms of rolls on a baking sheet. Top each roll bottom with beef and 2 slices cheese. Bake at 350 degrees for several minutes, until cheese melts. Add tops of rolls. Serve with reserved au jus in small bowls. Makes 6 sandwiches.

Allow a little extra time when slow-cooking in summertime... high humidity can cause food to take longer to finish cooking.

Moving-Day Sloppy Joes

Pam Hooley
LaGrange, IN

When we were moving, my neighbor offered to make a meal for us and the movers. This is what she brought. It was so good, I asked for the recipe, and have made it many times since. It's handy to have in the crockpot for home or travel.

3 lbs. ground beef
1 onion, chopped
10-3/4 oz. can cream of
    mushroom soup
10-3/4 oz. can tomato soup
1/2 c. rolled oats, uncooked
1/2 c. catsup
2 T. vinegar

1 T. Worcestershire sauce
1 T. mustard
1 t. salt
8-oz. pkg. pasteurized process
    cheese, cubed, or shredded
    Cheddar cheese
15 to 20 sandwich buns, split

Brown beef with onion in a large skillet over medium heat; drain. Add beef mixture to a 5-quart crockpot along with remaining ingredients except buns. Cover and cook on low setting for 4 to 6 hours, stirring occasionally. To serve, spoon beef mixture onto buns. Makes 15 to 20 sandwiches.

Crockpot sandwiches are so deliciously saucy! To keep juice from dripping, wrap individual servings in aluminum foil, then peel back as they're eaten.

CLASSIC CROCKPOT RECIPES

Game-Day Meatball Subs

April Jacobs
Loveland, CO

When my teens invite their friends over to watch the big game, this is always on the menu. Just add pickles and potato chips...it's game time!

1-1/2 lbs. lean ground beef
1 egg, lightly beaten
2/3 c. onion, finely chopped
1/3 c. dry bread crumbs
1 t. fresh oregano, chopped
1/2 t. salt
1/2 t. pepper
28-oz. can crushed tomatoes

2 T. brown sugar, packed
2 T. Dijon mustard
1 T. chili powder
1 t. garlic powder
8 hoagie rolls, split and toasted
1-1/2 c. shredded sharp Cheddar
   cheese

In a large bowl, combine beef, egg, onion, bread crumbs, oregano, salt and pepper. Mix well, using your hands. Form into 32 balls; arrange on an ungreased rimmed baking sheet. Bake at 350 degrees for 25 minutes; drain. Meanwhile, in a 4-quart crockpot, combine tomatoes with juice, brown sugar, mustard and seasonings; stir well. Add meatballs, pushing gently into sauce. Cover and cook on low setting for 3 to 4 hours. To serve, place several meatballs on each hoagie roll; top with sauce from crock and add cheese. Makes 8 sandwiches.

Pick up a stack of retro-style plastic burger baskets. Lined with crisp paper napkins, they're still such fun for serving hot dogs, burgers and fries. Don't forget the pickle!

Tailgate Beer Brats

Cindy Neel
Gooseberry Patch

*We all love these flavorful brats! They're so simple to fix, I have
plenty of time left to make potato salad and my famous
deviled eggs. Go team!*

19-oz. pkg. bratwurst sausages
1 yellow onion, sliced and
   separated into rings
2 T. butter, sliced

3 to 4 12-oz. cans regular or
   non-alcoholic beer
5 hoagie buns, split
Optional: chopped onions

Brown bratwursts in a heavy skillet over medium-high heat; drain. In
a 4-quart crockpot, combine onion rings and butter. Transfer brats to
crockpot; add enough beer to just cover brats. Cover and cook on high
setting for about 2 hours, until brats are cooked through. Serve brats on
buns, topped with onions, if desired. Makes 5 sandwiches.

Caramelized onions are delicious and easy to make. In a
crockpot, combine 1/2 cup butter, 3 pounds sliced sweet
onions and one teaspoon salt. Cover and cook on low setting
for 8 to 10 hours, stirring once or twice. Spoon onions
over sandwiches to add savory flavor.

Barbecued Pork Butt

Constance Lewis
Florence, AL

We enjoy this delicious pork either on buns, or by itself with sweet corn on the cob and baked potatoes.

5 to 6-lb. boneless or bone-in
    pork butt or shoulder roast
salt and pepper to taste
Optional: 1/8 to 1/4 t. cayenne
    pepper

1/4 c. apple juice or water
1 c. barbecue sauce
10 to 12 sandwich buns, split
Garnish: additional barbecue
    sauce

Add pork roast to a 6 to 7-quart crockpot, cutting roast to fit, if necessary. Season roast with salt, pepper and cayenne pepper, as desired; pour apple juice or water around roast. Cover and cook on low setting for 7 to 9 hours. Drain any excess liquid from crock. Shred pork with 2 forks, discarding excess fat and bone. Return pork to crock; top with barbecue sauce and stir to coat well. Cover and cook on low setting for another one to 2 hours. Serve pork on buns, with additional barbecue sauce on the side. Makes 10 to 12 sandwiches.

Sweet potato fries with a sandwich meal...deliciously different! Slice sweet potatoes into wedges, toss with olive oil and place on a baking sheet. Bake at 400 degrees for 20 to 30 minutes, until tender, turning once. Sprinkle with a little cinnamon-sugar and serve warm.

TAILGATE & PARTY SANDWICHES

24-Hour Italian Beef

Judy Phelan
Macomb, IL

My sister-in-law shared this recipe several years ago and it has been a family favorite since. It takes awhile, but requires little effort.

3 to 5-lb. beef rump roast
1-oz. pkg. Italian salad
   dressing mix

1-oz. pkg. au jus gravy mix
2 c. water
6 to 8 hard rolls, split

Place roast in a 6-quart crockpot; set aside. In a bowl, stir together mixes and water; spoon over roast. Cover and cook on low setting for 24 hours. (Don't peek!) Break up beef in crock after 12 to 15 hours. Serve beef mixture on rolls. Makes 6 to 8 sandwiches.

Crazy-Good Chicken

Leslie Nagel
Noxapater, MS

You can easily turn this into an appetizer...turn it into chicken sliders, using slider rolls! Delicious served over cooked rice, too.

4 boneless, skinless chicken
   breasts
1/2 t. garlic powder
16-oz. bottle zesty Italian
   salad dressing

16-oz. bottle honey barbecue
   sauce
6 sandwich buns, split

Spray a 5-quart crockpot with non-stick vegetable spray. Season chicken breasts with garlic powder; arrange in crock. Drizzle salad dressing and barbecue sauce over chicken. Cover and cook on low setting for 4 to 6 hours, until chicken is tender. Shred chicken with a fork; stir into sauce mixture. Spoon onto buns. Makes 6 sandwiches.

A properly working crockpot uses about as much electricity as a lightbulb, making it more economical (and cooler!) than using the stove.

Cheesesteak Sandwiches

Marsha Baker
Palm Harbor, FL

I fixed this for my beloved hubby for many Fathers' Days because it was always his favorite. The hardest part is slicing the steak, but the crockpot does most of the work for you.

1 lb. beef sirloin or round steak,
   thinly sliced
1/2 sweet onion, diced
1/2 red or yellow pepper, diced
Optional: 7-oz. can mushroom
   stems & pieces, drained
2 cloves garlic, minced
1/2 to 1 t. garlic powder

1 T. Worcestershire sauce or
   soy sauce
1 cube beef bouillon, crushed
1 T. butter, sliced
3 hoagie buns, split
Garnish: shredded
   Colby-Jack cheese

Spray a 4-quart crockpot with non-stick vegetable spray. Layer all ingredients except buns and garnish. Add enough water to barely cover steak. Cover and cook on low setting for 6 to 8 hours. When ready to serve, place steak mixture on buns using a slotted spoon; top with cheese and serve. Makes 3 sandwiches.

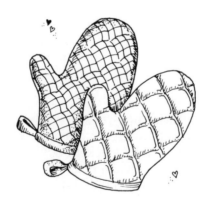

Keep a pair of long padded oven mitts nearby when slow cooking...they're perfect for lifting and carrying the hot crock safely.

TAILGATE & PARTY SANDWICHES

Joan's Beefy Sandwiches

Joan Chance
Houston, TX

Sure, you could use a canned Sloppy Joe sauce, but this recipe is simple and tasty. Total servings will depend on the size bun used, and how much is spooned onto each bun. Enjoy!

1-1/2 c. water
1/2 c. onion, finely chopped, or
    2 T. dried, minced onions
2 T. brown sugar, packed
2 T. cider vinegar
1 T. Worcestershire sauce

1 T. soy sauce
1 cube beef bouillon
1 cube chicken bouillon
3 lbs. ground beef, uncooked
6 to 8 burger or hot dog
    buns, split

In a 6-quart crockpot, combine all ingredients except beef and buns; mix well. Add beef, stirring to crumble. Cover and cook on low setting for 4 hours. Uncover; turn to high setting and cook to desired consistency, stirring occasionally. Serve on buns. Makes 8 sandwiches.

Hollowed-out peppers make garden-fresh servers for catsup, relish and mustard! Just cut a slice off the bottom so they'll sit flat.

CLASSIC CROCKPOT RECIPES

Mexican Shredded Chicken

Vickie
Gooseberry Patch

We love this juicy, tender chicken stuffed into taco shells, or for a change, into Mexican rolls called bolillos. Either way, they make a great meal. Garnish with your favorite cheese, diced tomatoes and shredded lettuce...serve with a chopped salad.

5 boneless, skinless chicken
    breasts
2 c. chunky salsa
2 T. ranch salad dressing mix

1 T. taco seasoning mix
8 taco shells or bolillos, split
Garnish: favorite toppings

Layer chicken breasts in a 5-quart crockpot. Top with salsa and seasoning mixes; mix gently. Cover and cook on low setting for 5 hours, or until chicken is very tender. Shred chicken with 2 forks; stir into salsa mixture in crock. To serve, spoon into taco shells or bolillos; garnish as desired. Makes 8 servings.

Serve a basket of warmed flour tortillas with Mexican Shredded Chicken. Simply wrap tortillas in aluminum foil and pop into a 250-degree oven for about 15 minutes...easy!

TAILGATE & PARTY SANDWICHES

Buffalo Chicken Sandwiches
Kelly Alderson
Erie, PA

A tasty change from Buffalo wings! I like to serve them with crisp celery sticks, blue cheese dip and potato chips.

4 boneless, skinless chicken
  breasts
16-oz. bottle Buffalo wing
  sauce, divided

1-1/2 T. ranch salad
  dressing mix
2 T. butter, sliced
6 hoagie rolls, split

Layer chicken breasts in a 5-quart crockpot; add one cup wing sauce and all the ranch dressing mix. Cover and cook on low setting for 6 to 7 hours. Shred chicken in crock with 2 forks; stir in butter. Spoon chicken and sauce into hoagie rolls; serve with remaining wing sauce. Makes 6 sandwiches.

Shredded Turkey Sandwiches
Karen Gierhart
Fremont, OH

These are easy sandwiches to make for graduations, showers and other festive occasions. Use a crockpot liner for easy clean-up!

6-oz. pkg. turkey or chicken
  stuffing mix
1 c. warm water
28-oz. can turkey breast

10-3/4 oz. can cream of
  mushroom soup
8 to 10 sandwich buns, split

In a 5-quart crockpot, combine dry stuffing mix and warm water; toss to mix well. Shred undrained turkey with a fork and spoon over stuffing; top with spoonfuls of mushroom soup. Cover and cook on low setting for 3 to 4 hours; stir after 2 hours. Serve turkey mixture spooned onto buns. Makes 8 to 10 sandwiches.

Just for fun, spear a cherry tomato or a tiny sweet pickle with a long party pick and use as a sandwich garnish.

CLASSIC CROCKPOT RECIPES

Maid Rites

Cheryl Culver
Coyle, OK

This is a very old recipe that makes the old fashioned loose-meat sandwiches like the Maid Rite restaurants used to have. We loved to go there and have dinner. The beef is steamed slowly, and crumbles with juicy flavors...a little sweet and a little tart. Add cheese slices, pickles and a favorite side, and this is an easy meal for a lot of folks.

1 c. warm water
2 T. light brown sugar, packed
2 T. cider vinegar
2 T. Worcestershire sauce
1 T. soy sauce
1 T. onion, minced

1 cube beef bouillon
1 cube chicken bouillon
3 lbs. ground beef, uncooked
8 hamburger buns, split
Garnish: cheese slices, pickles,
onions, lettuce

In a 6-quart crockpot, combine all ingredients except beef, buns and garnish; stir to mix. Add beef; stir until crumbled and completely coated. Cover and cook on high setting for one hour, stirring occasionally to break up beef. Uncover; continue cooking on low setting for 2-1/2 to 3 hours, until most of the liquid has cooked off, stirring occasionally. Serve on buns, using a slotted spoon; add desired toppings and serve. Makes 8 sandwiches.

For casual get-togethers, a wide roll of freezer paper is handy for covering tables. Before dinner, kids can have fun drawing on it with crayons...after dinner, just toss the paper or display their masterpieces!

TAILGATE & PARTY SANDWICHES

Root Beer Pulled Pork

Mel Chencharick
Julian, PA

I would have never thought of using root beer with pulled pork. It really gives it a good flavor. We like to toast the hamburger buns just a little. Pick your favorite root beer, and chill the rest to serve with dinner!

2-lb. pork tenderloin
12-oz. can root beer
18-oz. bottle favorite barbecue
 sauce

8 hamburger buns, split
 and toasted
small amount olive oil

Place pork tenderloin in a 4-quart crockpot; pour root beer over pork. Cover and cook on low setting for 6 to 7 hours, until well cooked and very tender. Pull and shred pork apart; return to crock and stir in barbecue sauce. Shortly before serving time, brush cut sides of hamburger buns with a little olive oil. Bake on a baking sheet at 250 degrees for 10 to 15 minutes, or toast on a grill for about 5 minutes, watching closely to avoid burning. Spoon pork onto buns and serve. Makes 8 servings.

Cooking for a crowd? Roasting meats can usually be doubled in a large crockpot. Add only half again as much seasoning, not twice as much...otherwise flavors may be too strong.

CLASSIC CROCKPOT RECIPES

Sweet Peppery Pork Tenderloin

Lisa Ashton
Aston, PA

I love to make dinner in the crockpot. Pork is always a favorite in our family! Made with blackberry jam and red wine vinegar, this is delicious.

1-1/2 lb. pork tenderloin
1/2 c. blackberry jam
2 T. red wine vinegar
1 t. garlic powder

1 t. salt
1 t. pepper
8 sandwich rolls, split

Place pork tenderloin in a 4-quart crockpot; set aside. In a small bowl, combine remaining ingredients except rolls; stir until smooth and spread over pork. Cover and cook on low setting for 6 hours, or until pork is tender. Shred pork using 2 forks; stir into mixture in crock and spoon onto rolls. Makes 8 sandwiches.

Asian-Inspired Pulled Pork

Nancy Kailihiwa
Wheatland, CA

Family dinners are important to us ever since my children have grown and gone off in different directions. Once a week, we get together at one of our homes to have dinner and catch up. I discovered this recipe by accidental when I was out of a staple in my pantry. It is now a favorite!

3 lbs. boneless country-style
   pork ribs
20-3/4 oz. bottle Asian honey
   sesame sauce, divided

4 to 6 hamburger buns, split
Optional: sliced cheese, favorite
   condiments

Layer ribs in a 5-quart crockpot; drizzle with half of honey sesame sauce. Cover and cook on low setting for 4 to 6 hours, until pork is fork-tender. Shred pork; transfer to a skillet over medium heat. Add remaining sauce and cook until edges of pork are crisp. Spoon pork into buns; serve with or without cheese and your favorite condiments. Makes 4 to 6 sandwiches.

FAVORITE POTLUCK SIDES

Calico Beans

Raksaa Meulenberg
Schenevus, NY

We love to serve these beans over rice. You can add some sliced hot dogs, if desired. I'm happy to share this family favorite for others to enjoy!

1 lb. ground beef
15-1/2 oz. can kidney
  beans, drained
15-1/2 oz. can black
  beans, drained
15-1/2 oz. can pinto
  beans, drained

1/2 c. brown sugar, packed
1/2 c. catsup
2 T. vinegar
1 T. mustard
1/2 t. salt

Brown beef in a skillet over medium heat; drain and add to a 4-quart crockpot. Carefully stir in beans; set aside. In a small bowl, mix together remaining ingredients; spoon over bean mixture and mix gently. Cover and cook on high setting for 5 to 6 hours. Stir again and serve. Makes 8 servings.

Make meals extra special for your family!
Pull out the good china and light some candles...
you'll be making memories together.

FAVORITE POTLUCK SIDES

Tina's Fried Apples

Tina Matie
Alma, GA

No skillet needed! These "fried" apples are so tender and full of flavor...an absolutely delicious recipe you can make in your crockpot. Scrumptious with roast pork!

3 to 4 lbs. Granny Smith or
   Golden Delicious apples,
   peeled, cored and cut
   into wedges
2 T. cornstarch
1/4 c. brown sugar, packed

1/4 c. sugar
1 t. cinnamon
1/4 c. butter, melted
2 t. lemon juice
1 t. vanilla extract

Add apples to a 6-quart crockpot; sprinkle with cornstarch and stir to coat apples. Sprinkle with sugars and cinnamon; stir to mix well. Stir in melted butter, lemon juice and vanilla. Cover and cook on high setting for 2 hours, or until apples are tender. Stir again and serve. Makes 8 servings.

Keep a shaker jar of apple pie spice handy if you love apple dishes. A blend of cinnamon, nutmeg and allspice, it's scrumptious in all kinds of recipes, from applesauce to pies to quick breads.

Au Gratin Potatoes

Georgia Muth
Penn Valley, CA

This easy recipe is great for the holidays when your oven is full with other dishes. For great flavor, I like to use Yukon Gold potatoes, but you can also use russets. Use a mandoline slicer to slice the potatoes, if you have one. I also shred my cheese rather than using cheese that's already shredded.

1/4 c. butter
1/4 c. all-purpose flour
2 c. whole milk
2 t. garlic powder
1 t. onion powder
1 t. salt
1/2 t. pepper

1 c. shredded Gruyère cheese
1 c. shredded sharp Cheddar
    cheese
3 lbs. Yukon Gold potatoes,
    peeled and sliced 1/8-inch
    thick

Melt butter in a large saucepan over medium-low heat; whisk in flour. Add milk and seasonings; whisk to combine. Continue to cook just until mixture begins to thicken, whisking frequently. Remove from heat; add cheeses and stir until melted. In a 4-quart crockpot coated with non-stick vegetable spray, layer 1/3 of potatoes and 1/3 of cheese sauce; repeat layering twice. Cover and cook on high setting for 3 to 4 hours, or on low setting for 4 to 6 hours, until potatoes are tender. Turn off crockpot; let stand, covered, for 20 minutes before serving to allow sauce to thicken. Makes 8 servings.

If you like crispy crumb toppings for casseroles, try this. Melt one tablespoon butter in a skillet over medium-high heat. Add one cup bread crumbs or crushed crackers; cook and stir until toasty. Season with garlic powder, salt and pepper... sprinkle over individual servings.

FAVORITE POTLUCK SIDES

Yellow Squash Casserole

Tracy Platt
Casselberry, FL

This side is good served with baked chicken or pork chops, and my kids love it. I got this recipe from a friend several years ago. If you don't care for cornbread stuffing, just use the kind you prefer.

4 c. yellow squash, thinly sliced
1/2 c. onion, chopped
1 c. carrots, peeled and shredded
10-3/4 oz. can cream of
    chicken soup

1 c. sour cream
1/4 c. all-purpose flour
6-oz. pkg. cornbread stuffing
    mix
1/2 c. butter, melted

In a large bowl, combine squash, onion, carrots and chicken soup; set aside. In another bowl, stir together sour cream and flour; stir into squash mixture. In a large bowl, toss stuffing mix with melted butter. Layer half of stuffing mixture in a 5-quart crockpot. Add vegetable mixture; spoon remaining stuffing mixture on top. Cover and cook on low setting for 7 to 9 hours, until hot and bubbly. Serves 6 to 8.

Try this easy substitute for canned cream soups. Combine one tablespoon softened butter, 3 tablespoons flour, 1/2 cup low-fat milk, 1/2 cup chicken broth, salt and pepper to taste. Blend well and use in place of one 10-3/4 ounce can of cream soup.

CLASSIC CROCKPOT RECIPES

Curried Rice & Lentils

Shirley Howie
Foxboro, MA

This is so quick & easy to prepare and makes a great side dish. It can also become a main dish with the addition of cooked and diced ham, pork or chicken. I just stir in any leftover meat I have on hand during the last hour of cooktime and I have a delicious one-pot dinner!

4 c. chicken broth
1 c. long-cooking white rice,
   uncooked
1/2 c. dried lentils, rinsed
   and sorted

3/4 c. onion, finely diced
2 to 3 t. curry powder, to taste
1 t. garlic powder
1/2 t. salt
1/4 t. pepper

Combine all ingredients in a 4-quart crockpot and stir well. Cover and cook on low setting for 4 to 5 hours, until rice and lentils are tender. Stir again and serve. Makes 6 servings.

Garnish slow-cooked dishes to add color and texture.
Diced red peppers, snipped fresh chives, crispy bacon,
chopped toasted nuts or a sprinkle of cheese are all good.

FAVORITE POTLUCK SIDES

Gran's Pinto Beans

Beckie Apple
Grannis, AR

My dear mother was a fantastic Southern cook. Our whole family grew up loving her home-cooked meals. Her crockpot pinto beans were the best! My son would say "Mom, can you cook Gran's beans for me?" There's nothing better, served with a pan of hot cornbread.

2 c. dried pinto beans, rinsed
   and sorted
6 slices bacon, cut into thirds
5 c. hot water

2 T. sugar
1 t. salt
1/2 t. pepper

Combine all ingredients in a 4-quart crockpot; stir gently. Cover and cook on high setting for 5 hours, or until beans are tender. Serves 4 to 6.

Crowd-Pleasing Creamed Corn

Laura Fredlund
Papillion, NE

*This side dish is easily the star at any gathering.
It's simply delicious...try it and see!*

32-oz. pkg. frozen corn
8-oz. pkg. cream cheese, cubed
1/4 c. butter, sliced

1/3 c. whipping cream
2 T. sugar
salt and pepper to taste

Combine all ingredients in a 4-quart crockpot; stir. Cover and cook on low setting for 4 hours, stirring occasionally. Serves 8.

Keep most-used recipes at your fingertips! Tack them to self-stick cork tiles placed inside a kitchen cabinet door.

CLASSIC CROCKPOT RECIPES

Garden Green Beans & Potatoes

Tina Goodpasture
Meadowview, VA

I've always enjoyed these two vegetables, and I like to experiment with both to find new ways to serve. This recipe is my favorite.

2 lbs. fresh green beans, trimmed
1-1/2 lbs. redskin potatoes,
    quartered
3/4 c. onion, chopped
1/2 c. beef broth
1 t. dried thyme

1-1/2 t. salt
1/2 t. pepper
1/2 c. butter, softened
1 T. lemon juice
Optional: crumbled bacon

In a 6-quart crockpot, combine green beans, potatoes, onion, beef broth and seasonings. Mix gently. Cover and cook on low setting for 6 to 8 hours, until vegetables are tender. Stir in butter and lemon juice. Top with crumbled bacon, if desired; serve with a slotted spoon. Makes 10 to 12 servings.

Surprisingly, potatoes and carrots can take longer to cook than meat. Add them to the crockpot first, and they'll cook faster.

FAVORITE POTLUCK SIDES

Veggies in Swiss Cheese Sauce

Liz Plotnick-Snay
Gooseberry Patch

Perfect for your Thanksgiving buffet...everyone loves it!

4 c. broccoli flowerets
4 c. cauliflower flowerets
1 c. onion, chopped
1-1/2 c. shredded Swiss cheese

15-oz. jar Alfredo sauce
1 t. dried thyme
1/4 t. pepper
Garnish: 1/2 c. slivered almonds

In a 4-quart crockpot, combine all ingredients except garnish; mix gently. Cover and cook on low setting for 6 to 7 hours, until vegetables are tender. Stir gently before serving. Sprinkle with almonds and serve. Makes 10 servings.

Table tents let everyone know what goodies are in potluck crockpots! Fold a piece of paper in half and jot down or rubber stamp the recipe name on the front...be sure to add the cook's name.

CLASSIC CROCKPOT RECIPES

Old-Fashioned Stuffing

Gladys Kielar
Whitehouse, OH

*This is a favorite at our family dinners. It cooks on
the countertop while the turkey roasts in the oven.*

12-oz. pkg. dried bread cubes
2 T. fresh parsley, chopped
1/2 t. salt
1/8 t. pepper
1/2 c. butter

1-1/2 c. celery, chopped
1/2 c. onion, chopped
2 eggs, beaten
1-1/2 c. milk

Combine bread cubes, parsley, salt and pepper in a 5-quart crockpot
coated with non-stick vegetable spray; set aside. Melt butter in a skillet
over medium heat. Sauté celery and onion until tender; add to bread
cubes along with eggs and milk. Stir together gently until well mixed.
Cover and cook on high setting for one hour. Stir; cover and cook
another 4 hours, or until heated through. Makes 6 servings.

Hosting a Thanksgiving dinner with all the trimmings?
With a crockpot, you can free up oven space by
preparing a savory slow-cooked side dish. Crockpots
are so handy, you may want more than one!

Brown Sugar-Glazed Carrots

Michelle Newlin
Portage, PA

A perfect side dish to complement any main dish!

2 lbs. carrots, peeled and sliced
    into 1/2-inch pieces
1/4 c. butter, melted
1/3 c. brown sugar, packed

1/4 t. cinnamon
1/8 t. nutmeg
1/2 t. salt
Garnish: chopped fresh parsley

Add carrots to a 4-quart crockpot; set aside. In a small bowl, whisk together melted butter, brown sugar and seasonings; spoon over carrots and toss to coat. Cover and cook on high setting for 3 hours, or until carrots are tender. For a thicker glaze, cover and cook on high setting for an additional 15 minutes. Sprinkle with parsley and serve. Makes 8 servings.

Cooked all day in a crockpot, root vegetables like potatoes, carrots and onions become tender and sweet. Give sweet potatoes and parsnips a try, too...they're delicious!

CLASSIC CROCKPOT RECIPES

Autumn Apples & Squash

Janis Parr
Ontario, Canada

This delicious fall dish is comfort food at its best.

1 butternut squash, peeled,
    seeded and cut into 1/2-inch
    cubes, divided
6 McIntosh apples, peeled, cored
    and cubed, divided
1 c. brown sugar, packed

2/3 c. butter, melted
3 T. all-purpose flour
1 t. cinnamon
1/2 t. ground ginger
1/4 t. nutmeg
1/4 t. salt

Layer half of squash in a buttered 6-quart crockpot; top with half of apples. Set aside; do not stir. Combine remaining ingredients in a bowl; mix with a fork until crumbly. Spread half of brown sugar mixture evenly over apples. Repeat layering with remaining squash, apples and brown sugar mixture. Cover and cook on low setting for 6 hours, or on high setting for 3-1/2 hours, until squash and apples are tender. Makes 6 to 8 servings.

Protect a favorite cookbook from cooking spatters...slip the opened book into a large plastic zipping bag before you begin.

FAVORITE POTLUCK SIDES

Spiced Applesauce

Lisa Smith
Huntington, IN

Scrumptious! You can use any good eating apple, but Golden Delicious apples are my favorite. This freezes nicely.

8 to 10 Golden Delicious
   apples, rinsed
1/2 c. water
3/4 c. sugar

1 t. cinnamon
1 t. ground cloves
1/2 t. nutmeg

Cut apples into medium chunks; no need to peel or core. Add to a 5-quart crockpot and drizzle with water. Mix together sugar and spices; sprinkle over apples and mix well. Cover and cook on low setting for 7 to 8 hours, until apples are very tender. Strain apple mixture through a food grinder, discarding cores and peels. Serve hot or cold. Makes 4 to 5 cups.

Fresh Cranberry Sauce

Jennie Gist
Gooseberry Patch

No muss, no fuss...and your home will smell wonderful!

1/2 c. orange juice
1/2 c. water
1/2 c. brown sugar, packed

1/2 c. sugar
1/4 t. cinnamon
12-oz. pkg. fresh cranberries

Combine orange juice, water, sugars and cinnamon in a 3-quart crockpot. Mix well; stir in cranberries. Cover and cook on high setting for 3 hours, stirring once each hour. Stir again. Cover and cook for another 45 minutes, or until thickened and most cranberries have popped. Serve warm or chilled. Serves 12.

Fresh cranberries can be kept frozen up to 12 months, so if you enjoy them, stock up when they're available in the fall and pop unopened bags in the freezer.

Spicy Black Beans

Chad Rutan
Gooseberry Patch

This is so simple, I make it for all of our favorite
south-of-the-border meals. Serve with hot cooked rice.

2 c. dried black beans, rinsed
    and sorted
5 c. vegetable broth
1 c. onion, chopped
1 c. celery, chopped
1 c. carrot, peeled and chopped
1 yellow or green pepper,
    chopped

2 jalapeño peppers, chopped
4 cloves garlic, minced
1 T. ground cumin
1 T. dried thyme
1/2 t. salt
1/4 t. pepper
2 bay leaves

Cover beans with water in a large bowl; let stand overnight. In the morning, drain; transfer beans to a 5-quart crockpot. Add remaining ingredients; mix well. Cover and cook on low setting for 8 to 10 hours, until beans are tender. Discard bay leaves. At serving time, mash beans slightly with a potato masher, if desired. Makes 8 servings.

Keep frozen chopped onions, peppers and veggie blends on hand for quick meal prep. They'll thaw quickly so you can assemble a recipe in a snap...no peeling, chopping or dicing!

FAVORITE POTLUCK SIDES

Red Beans & Rice

Carolyn Deckard
Bedford, IN

Great for your lucky New Year's Day bean dish! The red beans can be left to simmer in the crockpot while you are busy doing other things. Good with sliced green onions sprinkled on top.

7 c. water
16-oz. pkg. dried kidney beans,
   rinsed and sorted
1-1/2 c. green pepper, chopped
1 c. onion, chopped
2 cloves garlic, finely chopped

1-1/2 t. salt
1/4 t. pepper
2 c. instant rice, uncooked
Garnish: hot pepper sauce
   to taste

In a 5-quart crockpot, mix all ingredients except rice and hot sauce. Cover and cook on high setting for 4 to 5 hours, until beans are tender. Stir in uncooked rice. Cover and cook on high setting for 15 to 20 minutes, until rice is tender. Serve with hot sauce on the side. Makes 8 servings.

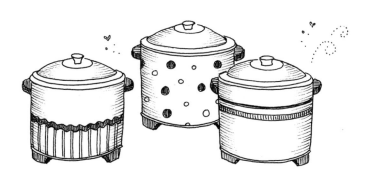

Bring the whole neighborhood together with a progressive crockpot dinner! Start at one end of the street with appetizers... finish at the other end with dessert. With crocks of food set on low or warm, everyone can go from house to house together without missing any of the fun or food.

CLASSIC CROCKPOT RECIPES

Spiced Butternuts & Pearls
Courtney Stultz
Weir, KS

This recipe can slow-cook all day and tastes great, without taking up oven or stove space. It's slightly spicy with a touch of sweetness. Great with holiday ham!

4 c. butternut squash, peeled, seeded and cut into 1/2-inch cubes
3 Granny Smith apples, peeled, cored and cut into 1/2-inch cubes
1 c. pearl onions, peeled and halved
1/4 c. brown sugar, packed
3 T. coconut oil or butter, melted
2 cloves garlic, minced
1/2 t. fresh ginger, peeled and minced
1/4 t. cayenne pepper
1/4 t. chili powder
1 t. sea salt
1/2 t. pepper

Combine all ingredients in a 5-quart crockpot; toss until well coated. Cover and cook on high setting for about 4 hours, or on low setting for about 8 hours, until squash and apples are tender. Makes 8 servings.

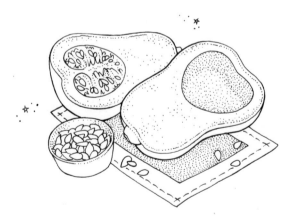

Add a crunchy, tasty topping to slow-cooked casseroles. Try finely crushed cheese crackers, herbed stuffing mix or even barbecue potato chips!

FAVORITE POTLUCK SIDES

Cheesy Potatoes for a Crowd

April Garner
Independence, KY

Yum! This recipe can easily be cut in half for a smaller crowd.

2 32-oz. pkgs. frozen diced
   potatoes, partially thawed
2 10-3/4 oz. cans cream of
   chicken soup
8-oz. pkg. shredded Cheddar
   cheese

3 c. whole milk
1 c. butter, melted
1/4 c. dried, minced onions,
   or more to taste
3-oz. pkg. real bacon bits
1 t. kosher salt

Combine all ingredients in a greased 6-quart crockpot; mix gently. Cover and cook on low setting for 4-1/2 to 5 hours, stirring occasionally, until bubbly and potatoes are tender. Makes 24 servings.

Cheesy Broccoli Bake

Sara Huntley
Dodge Center, MN

This has become a much-requested holiday favorite, and it's so easy!

16-oz. pkg. frozen chopped
   broccoli, thawed
6-oz. pkg. chicken-flavored
   stuffing mix

2 10-3/4 oz. cans Cheddar
   cheese soup

Mix all ingredients well in a 5-quart crockpot. Cover and cook on high setting for one to 2 hours, or on low setting for 3 to 4 hours, until hot and bubbly. Makes 6 servings.

With crockpots, sudden changes from cold to hot are a no-no. Don't set a hot crock on a cold surface... run only warm, not cold, wash water into a hot crock.

CLASSIC CROCKPOT RECIPES

Donna's Herbed Baby Potatoes

Donna Carter
Ontario, Canada

*A great side dish...so easy! This goes well with spare ribs,
baked ham and roast beef. Delicious! Add a shake of garlic powder,
if you really like garlic.*

4 to 4-1/2 lbs. new potatoes,
 cut in half as needed
2 T. olive oil
2 t. garlic, pressed
1 t. salt
1/4 t. pepper

1 T. fresh parsley, chopped,
 or 1 t. dried parsley
2 t. fresh chives or green onions,
 chopped
1/2 c. butter, cubed

In a 6-quart crockpot, combine potatoes with all ingredients except
butter; toss to coat well. Scatter cubed butter over potatoes. Cover and
cook on low setting for 6 to 7 hours, until potatoes are tender. Makes
6 servings.

Slow cooking at high altitude takes a little longer. Be sure to
allow an extra 30 minutes for each hour of cooking time
specified in the recipe.

Scrumptious Sweet Potatoes

Lisa Ann Panzino DiNunzio
Vineland, NJ

A simple to make, yet delicious side dish.

6 to 7 sweet potatoes, peeled and
    cut into chunks
1-1/2 T. cornstarch
1/4 c. butter, diced
1 c. brown sugar, packed
1 t. cinnamon

1/2 t. sea salt
1/4 c. water
3 T. pure maple syrup
juice of 1 orange
1 t. vanilla extract

Add sweet potatoes to a 5-quart crockpot; sprinkle with cornstarch and toss to coat well. Dot with butter; sprinkle with brown sugar, cinnamon and salt. Drizzle with remaining ingredients. Cover and cook on low setting for 3 to 4 hours, stirring once or twice, until potatoes are tender. Toss potatoes once more and transfer to a serving dish. Serves 6 to 8.

Part of the secret of success in life is to eat what you like
and let the food fight it out inside.
– Mark Twain

CLASSIC CROCKPOT RECIPES

Down-Home Green Beans

Karen Smith
Rock Hill, SC

Just wonderful! Reminds me of the way Granny cooked the green beans she grew in her garden. She'd make a big pan of cornbread to go with them.

5 c. chicken broth
2-1/2 lbs. fresh green beans,
   trimmed and cut into
   1-1/2 inch pieces
1 large red onion, sliced
3 T. sugar

3 T. white vinegar
2 T. garlic, minced
1 T. seasoned salt
1 T. pepper
8 slices bacon, coarsely chopped

In a 5-quart crockpot, combine all ingredients except bacon; mix well and set aside. In a skillet over medium heat, cook bacon for 3 to 5 minutes, until almost crisp but not fully cooked. Stir bacon into mixture in crockpot. Cover and cook on high setting for one hour. Turn crockpot down to low setting; cover and cook for 7 hours more. Serve in a large bowl, drizzled with some of the broth from crock. Makes 8 to 10 servings.

Jot down all your favorite, tried & true crockpot recipes for a new bride who's just learning to cook. Tuck them inside a brand-new crockpot...she'll love 'em both!

FAVORITE POTLUCK SIDES

Broccoli & Cheese Casserole
Teresa Verell
Roanoke, VA

*This recipe is a favorite that's always requested!
Serve to your hungry family and guests.*

20-oz. pkg. frozen broccoli
  flowerets
10-3/4 oz. can cream of
  chicken soup

1/2 c. white onion, chopped
2-1/2 c. shredded extra-sharp
  Cheddar cheese

Add broccoli, chicken soup and onion to a 4-quart crockpot; stir well. Cover and cook on high setting for 2-1/2 to 3-1/2 hours. Add cheese and stir to mix well. Cover and cook for an additional 30 minutes, or until cheese is melted. Serves 5.

Easy Cheesy Potatoes
Toni Groves
Walshville, IL

*I take this tasty dish to a lot of potlucks. I have learned to take along
copies of the recipe, because people always ask for it!*

8-oz. pkg. pasteurized process
  cheese, cubed
8-oz. container sour cream

6 T. butter, sliced
2-1/2 lbs. potatoes, peeled
  and quartered

Combine cheese, sour cream and butter in a 4-quart crockpot. Cover and cook on low setting for 30 minutes, or until cheese begins to melt. Meanwhile, in a saucepan, cover potatoes with water; cook over high heat until fork-tender. Drain; dice potatoes and add to cheese mixture. Mix well. Cover and cook on low setting for one to 2 hours, until cheese is completely melted. Serves 6 to 8.

For a clever centerpiece in a jiffy,
set a tall pillar candle in the
center of a seasonal wreath.

5-Bean Casserole

Diana Krol
Hutchinson, KS

*This is the perfect side dish for any family barbecue,
fried chicken dinner or fish fry! It can be made ahead of time
and any leftovers can be frozen.*

15-1/2 oz. can chili beans
15-3/4 oz. can pork & beans,
  drained
15-1/2 oz. can kidney beans,
  drained
15-1/2 oz. can butter beans,
  drained
14-1/2 oz. can cut green
  beans, drained

1/2 lb. bacon, diced
1/2 onion, chopped
1 jalapeño pepper, chopped
1 c. brown sugar, packed
2 c. catsup
1 t. chili powder
1/2 t. ground cumin

In a 6-quart crockpot, stir all beans together; set aside. In a large skillet over medium heat, cook bacon until crisp. Drain, reserving drippings in pan; add to bean mixture. Add onion and jalapeño pepper to drippings in skillet; cook until tender. Add brown sugar, catsup and spices to skillet; simmer for 3 to 4 minutes. Stir onion mixture into bean mixture in crock. Cover and cook on low setting for 5 to 6 hours, until hot and bubbly. Serves 8 to 10.

Crockpots make family reunion dinners so easy!
While dinner cooks, families can enjoy a game of
baseball, croquet or hide & seek, or just sit in
the shade catching up with one another.

Crockpot Mac & Cheese

Kristy Wells
Ocala, FL

This is one of those online recipes we happen upon that turns into a family favorite. It's super easy, the kids can help make it, and everyone loves how rich it tastes without being a lot of work. Serve on its own or alongside your favorite meal. You can change out the type of cheese to your liking, or use what you have on hand. I hope you enjoy it as much as we do!

16-oz. pkg. elbow macaroni,
    uncooked
3 c. shredded Cheddar cheese
4 c. whole milk

12-oz. can evaporated milk
salt and pepper to taste
8-oz. pkg. cream cheese,
    unwrapped

Spray the inside of a 6-quart crockpot with cooking spray. Add all ingredients except cream cheese; stir gently until macaroni is covered by milk. Set block of cream cheese in the center. Cover and cook on high setting for 2 to 2-1/2 hours, stirring every 30 minutes, until macaroni is tender. Makes 6 to 8 servings.

Wrap and freeze small amounts of leftover cheeses.
They may become crumbly when thawed, but will still
be delicious in crockpot recipes.

CLASSIC CROCKPOT RECIPES

Donna's Great Beans

Donna Clement
Daphne, AL

Whenever I make this recipe, it reminds me of when my boys were little and we had to spend many a cold night out at the ball field. The concession stand always had the beans going, served with hot cornbread, to keep our innards warmed up. Delicious!

2 15-oz. cans pork & beans
16-oz. can large butter beans
15-1/2 oz. can kidney beans
1/2 lb. ground beef
1 onion, chopped

1/2 lb. bacon
3/4 c. brown sugar, packed
2 T. white vinegar
1 t. mustard
1/2 t. Worcestershire sauce

Add all undrained cans of beans to a 6-quart crockpot; set aside. Brown beef with onion in a skillet over medium heat; drain and add to beans. In the same skillet, cook bacon over medium heat until crisp; drain, crumble and add to beans. Stir in remaining ingredients. Cover and cook on low setting for 3 hours, or on high setting for 2 hours, stirring often. Makes 8 to 10 servings.

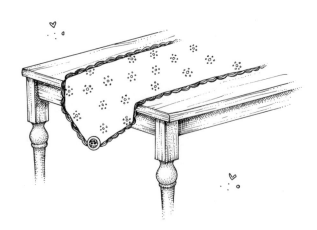

Create a table runner...a quick way to make any dinner more festive! Purchase cotton fabric in a cheerful seasonal print, hem or pink the edges and you're done!

FAVORITE POTLUCK SIDES

Jill's Creamy Corn Casserole

Jill Ball
Highland, UT

The last thing I want to do is spend Christmas day in the kitchen! This is an easy, yummy side dish that has become a Christmas dinner regular.

2 16-oz. pkgs. frozen corn
2 t. sugar
1 c. milk
1 t. salt
1/4 c. butter, cubed

8-oz. pkg. cream cheese, cubed
1/4 t. pepper
Optional: 8 slices crisply cooked, crumbled bacon, 1/3 c. sliced fresh chives

Combine frozen corn, sugar, milk and salt in a 5-quart crockpot; stir. Top with butter and cream cheese. Cover and cook on high setting for 2 to 3 hours, or on low setting for 4 to 5 hours. Stir; add pepper and stir again. If desired, top with bacon and chives at serving time. Makes 8 servings.

Serve up a fresh-tasting, crunchy salad your family will love. Simply toss together packaged salad greens with add-ins like raisins or dried cranberries, cheese crumbles and a favorite bottled salad dressing.

CLASSIC CROCKPOT RECIPES

Beckie's Tasty Potatoes

*Beckie Apple
Grannis, AR*

*These potatoes are the easiest to make! They are a perfect side
with any meal for any season. Love to get it going,
and four hours later, it's ready to serve.*

2 lbs. new Yukon Gold potatoes
3 T. oil
2 T. onion, diced

2 cloves garlic, pressed
3/4 t. salt
1/2 t. pepper

Combine all ingredients in a one-gallon plastic zipping bag. Seal; toss
to coat potatoes. Add potato mixture to a 5-quart crockpot. Cover and
cook on high setting for 4 hours, or until potatoes are fork-tender.
Serves 4 to 6.

No-Fuss Corn on the Cob

*Tina Matie
Alma, GA*

*This is the easiest way to cook corn on the cob! Perfect corn, every
time. Using the crockpot helps free up stove space when I am making
a big meal. Save time with pre-cut sheets of aluminum foil.*

8 to 12 ears sweet corn, husked
and silk removed

salt, pepper and butter to taste

Wrap each ear of corn in a square of aluminum foil. Lay corn in layers
in a 6-quart crockpot. Cover and cook on high setting for 2 hours, or on
low setting for 4 hours. Corn will steam inside the foil. Unwrap
carefully; season corn generously with salt, pepper and a few pats of
butter. Makes 8 to 12 servings.

Mix up some scrumptious herb butter for corn on the cob! Blend
1/2 cup softened butter with one teaspoon lemon juice and
one tablespoon each of chopped fresh chives and dill. Yum!

BUSY-DAY MAINS

Cheeseburger Potato Casserole

Joyce Roebuck
Jacksonville, TX

This is a good and easy one-dish recipe...great when you have friends over for a casual meal. Add a tossed green salad and your dinner is complete. Enjoy!

1 lb. ground beef
1/2 c. onion, chopped
10-3/4 oz. can Cheddar
   cheese soup
1/4 c. sweet pickle relish
2 T. brown mustard
2 T. catsup
1 T. Worcestershire sauce
30-oz. pkg. frozen shredded
   hashbrowns, thawed
   and divided

8-oz. pkg. shredded Cheddar
   cheese, divided
1 t. salt, divided
1/2 t. pepper, divided
Optional: additional catsup,
   sliced green onions

Brown beef with onion in a large skillet over medium-high heat, stirring to break up beef. Drain. Stir in cheese soup, relish, mustard, catsup and Worcestershire sauce until well blended; set aside. Add half of potatoes to a 5-quart crockpot sprayed with non-stick vegetable spray. Spoon half of beef mixture over potatoes; sprinkle with 1-1/2 cups cheese, 1/2 teaspoon salt and 1/4 teaspoon pepper. Repeat beef and potato layers; top with remaining cheese, salt and pepper. Cover and cook on low setting for 4 hours, or on high setting for 2 hours, until hot and bubbly. Top with additional catsup and green onions, if desired. Serves 6.

A rainy-day cure-all...toss together ingredients for a tasty crockpot meal, make some popcorn and enjoy a family movie marathon. When you're ready for dinner, it's ready for you!

Beef Tips & Rice

Anita Gibson
Hudson, WI

I loved making beef tips over rice, but I needed a quicker and tasty option. So I simplified a recipe, and now it's quick to prepare as well as delicious. Put it in the crockpot, and come home to wonderful aromas! Many compliments have been received on this.

2 lbs. stew beef cubes
1/2 c. onion, chopped
1 c. water
10-3/4 oz. can cream of
   mushroom soup

2 0.87-oz. pkgs. brown
   gravy mix
1 cube beef bouillon
cooked rice or noodles

Combine all ingredients except rice or noodles in a 4-quart crockpot; mix to combine. Cover and cook on low setting for 7 to 8 hours, until beef is tender. Stir again; serve over cooked rice or noodles. Makes 4 servings.

Pick up a bunch of fresh flowers on your next trip to the grocery store! Even the simplest bouquet of daisies tucked into a pitcher adds cheer to the dinner table.

CLASSIC CROCKPOT RECIPES

Tex-Mex Chicken

Amy Theisen
Sauk Rapids, MN

Add some cayenne pepper for extra zip...serve with crunchy tortilla chips and you have a winner of a dinner!

2 T. taco seasoning mix
2 T. all-purpose flour
1 lb. boneless, skinless chicken
    breasts, cut into 1-inch strips
1-1/2 c. thick & chunky salsa
1 green pepper, cut into
    1-inch strips

1 red pepper, cut into
    1-inch strips
1 c. frozen corn
3/4 c. canned black beans
cooked rice
Garnish: shredded Mexican-
    blend cheese

Mix taco seasoning mix and flour in a 4-quart crockpot. Add chicken strips; toss to coat well. Stir in salsa, peppers, corn and beans. Cover and cook on low setting for 6 to 8 hours, or on high setting for 3 to 4 hours, until chicken is tender. Serve over cooked rice, topped with cheese. Makes 4 servings.

Easy Chicken Tacos

Ann Farris
Biscoe, AR

This is so easy, and so good...it's all about the toppings with these tacos! I like to squeeze a lime over them.

1 lb. boneless, skinless chicken
    breasts
3 T. taco seasoning mix
1 c. chicken broth
6 tortillas or taco shells

Garnish: black beans, diced
    tomatoes, cubed avocado,
    sour cream, shredded
    Cheddar cheese

Add chicken breasts to a 4-quart crockpot; sprinkle with taco seasoning and toss to coat well. Add chicken broth. Cover and cook on low setting for 6 to 8 hours, until chicken is very tender. Using 2 forks, shred chicken in crock; stir well. Serve on flour tortillas or crunchy taco shells, garnished as desired. Serves 6.

Cut chicken into thin strips or slices in a snap.
Just freeze for 20 to 30 minutes before slicing.

BUSY-DAY MAINS

Angel Chicken

Charlotte Smith
Huntingdon, PA

I was given this recipe when searching for new ideas for supper.
It's a keeper...you will make it over and over. It's super easy!
Serve over rice, if you like.

2 lbs. boneless, skinless
   chicken breasts
2 10-3/4 oz. cans cream of
   chicken soup
1 c. white wine or chicken broth

8-oz. pkg. cream cheese, cubed
1/2 c. butter, sliced
2 0.7-oz. pkgs. Italian salad
   dressing mix

Layer chicken in a 5-quart crockpot; set aside. Combine remaining
ingredients in a large saucepan. Cook and stir over medium-low heat
until smooth and well blended. Remove from heat and spoon over
chicken. Cover and cook on high setting for 4 hours. Reduce setting
to low; cook for 2 additional hours. Shred chicken; stir into mixture
in crock and serve. Makes 6 to 8 servings.

A fresh and speedy side for a slow-cooker meal...
toss steamed green beans, broccoli or zucchini with
a little olive oil and chopped fresh herbs.

CLASSIC CROCKPOT RECIPES

Ranch Hands' Beefy Stew

Rena Tauck
Hammond, MT

*This is a hearty meal I fix for the ranch hands...
it is always a hit at potlucks!*

6 potatoes, peeled and sliced
6 carrots, peeled and sliced
2 lbs. ground beef, browned
   and drained
3/4 t. onion powder

1/2 t. salt
1 t. pepper
23-oz. can tomato soup
10-oz. pkg. frozen peas

In a 6-quart crockpot, layer 1/2 each of potatoes, carrots and beef, sprinkling each layer with seasonings. Spoon tomato soup over beef; top with peas. Cover and cook on high setting 4 to 5 hours; do not stir until serving time. Serves 8 to 10.

Chicken in Spicy Sauce

Tammy Navarro
Littleton, CO

My sister Pam gave this to me many years ago. It's a quick & easy meal that cooks all day, and supper's ready when you get home! Serve over cooked rice, with tossed salad and naan bread on the side.

1/2 c. brown sugar, packed
1/2 c. tomato juice
1/2 c. soy sauce
1/4 c. chicken broth

3 cloves garlic, minced
4 to 6 boneless, skinless chicken
   breasts

Combine all ingredients except chicken in a large bowl; mix well. Using tongs, dip each chicken breast into sauce; add chicken to a 6-quart crockpot coated with non-stick vegetable spray. Spoon remaining sauce over chicken. Cover and cook on low setting for 6 to 8 hours, or on high setting for 3 to 4 hours, until chicken is tender. Serves 4 to 6.

Prop a mini chalkboard next to the crockpot...it's just right for announcing what's for dinner and what time it will be ready.

BUSY-DAY MAINS

Dad's Laid-Off Chicken

Heather Porter
Villa Park, IL

A few years ago, my husband was laid off from his construction job. He was never much of a cook, but he decided one day to take out the crockpot and attempt a dinner. I had all of the ingredients in the freezer, fridge and pantry. It was a huge success! Serve over cooked rice or egg noodles...both ways are delicious! Reheats very well, too.

4 boneless, skinless chicken
 breasts
10-3/4 oz. can cream of
 chicken soup
10-3/4 oz. can cream of
 mushroom soup

10-3/4 oz. can cream of
 celery soup
7-1/2 oz. container garden
 vegetable cream cheese
cooked rice or egg noodles

Place chicken breasts in a 5-quart crockpot; spoon soups over chicken. Cover and cook on low setting for 6 hours, or until chicken is very tender. Shred chicken in the crock; stir in cream cheese. Cover and cook for another 30 minutes. Serve over cooked rice or noodles. Makes 6 servings.

It's not how much we have, but how much
we enjoy, that makes happiness.
– Charles Haddon-Spurgeon

Savory Stuffed Peppers

Jamie Plichta
North Huntingdon, PA

*This is a quick & easy recipe I like to toss together before work.
I love coming home to the delicious smell of dinner!
These may be served with a side of mashed potatoes.*

14-1/2 oz. can stewed tomatoes
2 15-oz. cans tomato sauce,
   divided
1 lb. ground beef
1/2 t. dried oregano
1-1/2 t. salt

1/2 t. pepper
8.8-oz. pkg. precooked rice
4 to 6 red, yellow and/or orange
   peppers, tops cut off and
   seeds removed

Add stewed tomatoes with juice and 3/4 of one can of tomato sauce to a 6-quart crockpot; set aside. In a bowl, season uncooked beef with oregano, salt and pepper. Mix in rice and remaining tomato sauce. Spoon beef mixture evenly into peppers; arrange peppers in crockpot. Cover and cook on low setting for 7 to 9 hours, until beef is cooked and peppers are tender. Makes 4 to 6 servings.

When trying a new-to-you crockpot recipe, it's a good idea
to stay nearby and check on it occasionally. That way,
you'll know exactly how long the recipe takes
to cook in your crockpot.

BUSY-DAY MAINS

Chicken & Rice with Mushrooms

Beckie Apple
Grannis, AR

Busy days bring out my crockpot, and this chicken & rice is a great meal plan on those days. Add a salad and bread...dinner is ready!

1-1/2 c. jasmine rice, uncooked
14-1/2 oz. can chicken broth
1-1/2 c. hot water
6 boneless, skinless chicken
   thighs

salt and pepper to taste
10-3/4 oz. can cream of
   mushroom soup
4-oz. can sliced mushrooms
1/4 c. onion, chopped

Spread uncooked rice in a 5-quart crockpot; add chicken broth and hot water. Season chicken thighs on both sides with salt and pepper; layer in crock. Add mushroom soup and mushrooms with liquid; top with onion. Cover and cook on high setting for 4 to 5 hours, until chicken is fork-tender. Makes 4 to 6 servings.

Simple crockpot recipes are ideal for older children just learning to cook. With supervision, kids can learn to use paring knives, can openers and hot mitts...and they'll be oh-so happy to serve the dinner they've prepared!

Salsa Chicken & Beans

Wendy Polley
Miamisburg, OH

A really easy, really delicious family-pleasing meal. My whole family enjoys this! Serve with cooked rice, or roll up in tortillas.

1-1/2 lbs. boneless, skinless
   chicken breasts
1-oz. pkg. taco seasoning mix
15-1/2 oz. can black beans,
   drained and rinsed

24-oz. jar favorite salsa
Optional: shredded Cheddar or
   Mexican-blend cheese

Layer all ingredients except optional cheese in a 5-quart crockpot. Cover and cook on high setting for 3 to 3-1/2 hours, or on low setting for 6 to 7 hours, until chicken is very tender. Remove chicken and shred; return to mixture in crock. Top with cheese, if desired. Makes 4 to 6 servings.

Serve up some "fried" ice cream with a Mexican feast. Freeze scoops of ice cream, roll in crushed frosted corn flake cereal and drizzle with honey. Top with cinnamon, whipped cream and a cherry. Yum!

BUSY-DAY MAINS

Nacho Chicken & Rice

Linda Peterson
Mason, MI

A delicious meal that my family loves!

1 lb. boneless, skinless chicken
   breasts, cubed
2 10-3/4 oz. cans Cheddar
   cheese soup

16-oz. jar chunky salsa
1-1/4 c. long-cooking rice,
   uncooked
1-1/4 c. water

Add all ingredients to a 5-quart crockpot and mix well. Cover and cook on low setting for 3 to 5 hours, stirring occasionally, until chicken is tender. Makes 4 servings.

Fiesta Ranch Pork

Melissa Woodson
Pasadena, TX

This recipe is on regular rotation in my home. My whole family loves it! My go-to is to shred and serve over rice, with a veggie on the side, usually steamed broccoli. It can also be spooned into buns. If you want to kick up the flavor, use two packets of the ranch mix.

2-lb. boneless pork roast
2 10-3/4 oz. cans cream of
   mushroom soup

1.1-oz. pkg. fiesta ranch dip mix
cooked rice or noodles

Place roast in a 4-quart crockpot; set aside. In a bowl, stir together mushroom soup and ranch mix; spoon over roast. Cover and cook on low setting for 7 to 8 hours. Shred roast and stir into soup mixture in crock. Serve over cooked rice or noodles. Serves 5 to 6.

Economical cuts of pork are perfect for slow cooking...
boneless shoulder roast, blade roast and country-style ribs.

Pizza Noodles

Agnes Ward
Ontario, Canada

Kids of all ages love this! If you want to cut down on fat, use ground turkey, turkey pepperoni and less cheese. It'll still be yummy!

12-oz. pkg. wide egg noodles, uncooked
1-1/2 lbs. ground beef
1/4 c. onion, chopped
26-oz. jar spaghetti sauce
4-oz. jar sliced mushrooms, drained
1-1/2 t. Italian seasoning
3-1/2 oz. pkg. pepperoni slices, cut in half
3 c. shredded mozzarella cheese, divided
3 c. shredded Cheddar cheese, divided

Cook noodles according to package directions, just until tender; drain. Meanwhile, in a skillet, cook beef with onion until no longer pink; drain. Stir in spaghetti sauce, mushrooms and seasoning. In a lightly greased 6-quart crockpot, spread 1/3 of beef mixture; top with 1/3 of noodles, all of pepperoni and 1/3 of both cheeses. Repeat layering twice, ending with cheeses. Cover and cook on low setting for 3 to 4 hours, until heated through and cheeses are melted. Makes 6 to 8 servings.

A crisp green salad goes well with all kinds of dinners. For a zippy citrus dressing, shake up 1/2 cup olive oil, 1/3 cup lemon or orange juice and a tablespoon of Dijon mustard in a small jar to blend, and chill.

Franks & Cheese

John Long
Grayland, WA

My family like hot dogs as well as macaroni & cheese. This is a way to enjoy both at once. It's so good, and easy to eat! "Queso blanco" style process cheese can be used for variety. This is a rich-tasting dish...use half the cheese, if preferred.

32-oz. pkg. 2% milk pasteurized process cheese, cubed
16-oz. pkg. elbow macaroni, uncooked
1-1/2 c. fat-free milk
12-oz. can evaporated milk

16-oz. pkg. turkey franks, sliced into round pieces
1 to 1-1/2 c. shredded Cheddar cheese
pepper to taste

Combine cubed cheese, uncooked macaroni and milks in a 6-quart crockpot. Add franks and shredded cheese; season with pepper. Cover and cook on low setting for 2 to 3 hours, or on high setting for 1-1/2 to 2 hours, until bubbly and cheese is melted. Stir and serve. Makes 8 to 10 servings.

Keep a basket packed with paper plates, napkins and cups. You'll be ready for a family picnic at a moment's notice... just grab dinner in the crockpot and go!

CLASSIC CROCKPOT RECIPES

Old-Fashioned Chicken & Gravy

Joan Raven
Cicero, NY

*Comfort food at its best...tender chicken with a savory gravy
that's perfect over mashed potatoes or egg noodles.*

3 to 4 boneless, skinless
   chicken breasts
1 t. garlic powder
sea salt to taste
1 t. pepper
2 14-1/2 oz. cans chicken broth
10-3/4 oz. can cream of
   chicken soup
10-3/4 oz. can cream of
   celery soup
2 0.87-oz. pkgs. brown
   gravy mix
1/4 c. all-purpose flour
mashed potatoes or cooked
   egg noodles

Pat chicken breasts dry; sprinkle with seasonings. Arrange chicken in
a 5-quart crockpot; set aside. Combine remaining ingredients except
potatoes or noodles in a bowl; stir well and spoon over chicken. Cover
and cook on high setting for 3 to 4 hours, or on low setting for 6 to
7 hours, until chicken is tender. At serving time, shred chicken into
bite-size pieces; stir into gravy in crock. Serve chicken and gravy over
mashed potatoes or cooked noodles. Makes 6 servings.

Easiest-ever iced tea...ready when you are! Start dinner in
the crockpot, then fill up a 2-quart pitcher with water and
add 8 tea bags. Cover and refrigerate for 6 to 10 hours.
At dinnertime, discard tea bags. Add sugar to taste
and serve over ice.

BUSY-DAY MAINS

Andy's Favorite Ribs

Tiffany Jones
Batesville, AR

My husband Andy loves ribs! I never had any luck cooking tender, fall-off-the-bone ribs, until I found a recipe similar to this one. I tweaked the dry rub to make it more to his taste and boy, did he love it. He told me this recipe was a keeper!

2 t. smoked paprika
2 t. seasoned salt
1 t. garlic powder
1 t. onion powder

salt and pepper to taste
3 to 4 lbs. pork baby back ribs
18-oz. bottle favorite barbecue
  sauce

Combine all seasonings in a bowl; mix well and rub over both sides of ribs. Spray a 6-quart crockpot with non-stick vegetable spray. Arrange ribs on their side, curving around the inside of crock; spoon barbecue sauce over ribs. Add a little water to sauce bottle; shake well and add to crock. Cover and cook on low setting for 8 hours, or until ribs are tender. If possible, flip the ribs over after 4 hours; baste with liquid in crock and finish cooking. Makes 6 servings.

Napkins are a must when juicy ribs are on the menu!
Glue wooden alphabet letter initials to plain napkin
rings and tuck in large-size cloth napkins.

Lasagna in the Crock

Mary Little
Franklin, TN

It's wonderful to come home to your aroma-filled kitchen on a cold evening. I love this with a tossed salad and homemade bread.

32-oz. container ricotta cheese
1 c. grated Parmesan cheese
8-oz. pkg. shredded mozzarella
  cheese, divided
1 egg, beaten
1/4 c. fresh basil, chopped

1 t. Italian seasoning
salt and pepper to taste
2 24-oz. jars marinara sauce,
  divided
12-oz. pkg. no-boil lasagna
  noodles, uncooked

In a bowl, stir together ricotta and Parmesan cheeses, one cup mozzarella cheese, egg and seasonings; set aside. Spread 1-1/2 cups marinara sauce in the bottom of a 6-quart crockpot. Top with 3 noodles, breaking to fit crock. Spoon 1/3 of cheese mixture over noodles. Top with another layer of sauce, noodles and cheese mixture. Repeat layers for a total of 3 layers. Top with remaining mozzarella cheese. Cover and cook on high setting for 3 to 4 hours, or on low setting for 6 to 8 hours, until hot and bubbly. Makes 6 to 8 servings.

A whimsical centerpiece for an Italian dinner! Take a handful of long pasta like spaghetti, bucatini or curly strands of fusilli, and fan it out in a wide-mouthed vase.

BUSY-DAY MAINS

Sweet-and-Sour Chicken

Cindy Sheets
Perkins, OK

This is the easiest recipe I have, but it doesn't taste simple.
My kids always loved it, too. I sometimes substitute the chicken
with pork chops. Serve over steamed rice with a crisp salad.

4 boneless, skinless
  chicken breasts
18-oz. jar apricot preserves

1 c. Russian salad dressing
1.35-oz. pkg. onion soup mix

Spray a 4-quart crockpot with non-stick vegetable spray. Layer chicken breasts in crock; set aside. Combine remaining ingredients in a bowl; mix well and spoon over chicken. Cover and cook on high setting for 4 hours, or until chicken is tender. Serves 4.

Pizza Chicken

Lisa Tucker
Dunbar, WV

This is one of the few crockpot meals that I knew everyone in
my family would enjoy. Even my picky kids would eat this!
I usually double the recipe. A zesty salad is a good side dish.

3 boneless, skinless
  chicken breasts
1 c. pizza sauce
1 c. shredded mozzarella cheese

9 pepperoni slices, or more
  to taste
Optional: other favorite pizza
  toppings

Arrange chicken in a 4-quart crockpot; spoon pizza sauce evenly over chicken. Sprinkle 1/3 cup cheese onto each chicken breast. Top with pepperoni and desired toppings. Cover and cook on high setting for 2 to 3 hours, until chicken is tender. Makes 3 servings.

Beef Over Noodles

Bootsie Dominick
Suches, GA

My husband Wyatt likes this a lot and it's easy to make. This is a great meal to serve in fall or winter with warm crusty bread. It makes the house smell wonderful while it cooks!

1/2 c. to 3/4 c. all-purpose flour	10-3/4 oz. can cream of
2 t. salt	mushroom soup
1/4 t. pepper	1.35-oz. pkg. onion soup mix
2 to 3 lbs. stew beef cubes	1/2 c. sour cream
2 T. oil	cooked flat egg noodles

Combine flour, salt and pepper in a large plastic zipping bag. Add beef cubes in small batches; shake to coat. Heat oil in a large skillet over medium heat. working in batches, add beef and brown on all sides. Transfer beef to a 5-quart crockpot. Mix together mushroom soup and onion soup mix; spoon over beef. Cover and cook on low setting for 6 to 8 hours. At serving time, stir in sour cream. Serve over cooked noodles. Makes 6 to 8 servings.

Longing for Mom's homemade egg noodles? Try frozen egg noodles. Thicker and heartier than dried noodles, these homestyle noodles cook up quickly in all your favorite recipes.

October Sausage Supper

Julie Dawson
Prospect Heights, IL

Perfect to toss together before going apple-picking in the fall. I like to use red pepper-infused oil when I sauté the sausage. Enjoy with a crisp salad and rye bread.

1 lb. smoked pork sausage link,
   cut into 1/2-inch slices
1 T. oil
14-1/2 oz. can diced tomatoes

28-oz. can sauerkraut, drained
1 onion, chopped
1 green pepper, chopped
1 T. garlic, minced

In a skillet over medium heat, sauté sausage in oil. Drain and transfer to a greased 4-quart crockpot. Add tomatoes with juice and remaining ingredients; mix gently. Cover and cook on low setting for 6 to 8 hours. Makes 4 to 6 servings.

When cooking cabbage or sauerkraut, try this
old trick...lay a heel of bread on top before covering
the pot, and there will be no cabbage odor!
Afterwards, just toss out the bread.

CLASSIC CROCKPOT RECIPES

Herbed Roast Chicken

Cheryl Culver
Perkins, OK

Once you've tried this, you'll never need to pick up a deli chicken at the store again! It's juicy, tender and easy. Serve it for dinner, or keep it in the fridge for making delicious sandwiches.

1 T. kosher salt
1 t. smoked paprika
1 t. onion powder
1 t. garlic powder
1 t. Italian seasoning
1/2 t. dried thyme
1/2 to 1 t. cayenne pepper

1/2 t. pepper
3-1/2 to 4-lb. whole chicken, cut
   into quarters
1 yellow onion, quartered
1 lemon, halved or quartered
3 to 4 cloves garlic, peeled

Combine all seasonings in a bowl; rub over all sides of chicken. Place chicken in a lightly greased 6-quart crockpot, skin-side down. Tuck onion, lemon and garlic around chicken. Cover and cook on high setting for 4 to 5 hours, or on low setting for 7 to 8 hours, until chicken is tender. If a more golden color is desired, transfer to a broiler pan; broil for a few minutes, until golden. Makes 6 servings.

For favorite recipes that you make often, mix up several small bags of the seasonings. Label with the recipe's name and tuck in the cupboard...a terrific time-saver for future meals!

BUSY-DAY MAINS

Ginger Ale Roast Beef

Liz Sulak
Rosenberg, TX

*This roast is one of the few meals that everyone in my family likes.
Serve with mashed potatoes, topped with gravy from the crock.*

3-lb. beef sirloin tip roast
1/2 c. all-purpose flour, divided
1.35-oz. pkg. onion soup mix

0.87-oz. pkg. brown gravy mix
2 c. ginger ale

Coat roast with half of flour; place roast in a 4-quart crockpot. Combine remaining flour, seasoning mixes and ginger ale; pour over roast. Cover and cook on low setting for 8 to 10 hours, until roast is very tender. Slice or shred and serve. Makes 6 servings.

Round Steak with Rich Gravy

Lynda Reaves
Carl Junction, MO

*A day with small children is a very busy day...this is an easy dinner
to get on the table! Serve with mashed potatoes and a green salad,
along with warm biscuits...you won't be disappointed!*

2-1/2 lbs. beef round steak, cut
   into serving-size pieces
10-3/4 oz. can cream of
   mushroom soup

1.35-oz. pkg. onion soup mix
1/4 c. water

Arrange steak pieces in a 4-quart crockpot; top with remaining ingredients. Cover and cook on low setting for 6 to 8 hours. Stir and serve. Makes 4 servings.

All-day slow cooking works wonders on less-tender, less-expensive cuts of beef...chuck, rump and arm roast, round steak and stew beef cook up juicy and delicious.

CLASSIC CROCKPOT RECIPES

Winner, Winner, Chicken & Noodle Dinner

Dian Bentley
Dresden, OH

Early in the morning, prepare this dish easily and let your crockpot do the rest! You'll have a delicious meal waiting for you at the end of the day.

4 to 6 boneless, skinless
   chicken breasts
16-oz. pkg. frozen egg noodles,
   uncooked
10-3/4 oz. can cream of
   chicken soup
10-3/4 oz. can cream of
   mushroom soup
1-1/4 c. milk
2 cubes chicken bouillon
1/2 c. seasoned dry bread
   crumbs

Layer chicken breasts in a 6-quart crockpot; add frozen noodles and set aside. In a bowl, whisk together soups and milk; spoon over noodles. Add bouillon cubes; push down into liquid. Sprinkle bread crumbs on top. Cover and cook on low setting for 6 hours, or until chicken is tender. Makes 4 to 6 servings.

While supper simmers in the crockpot, there's time to do other things. Why not bake up a double batch of cookies? There will be plenty for dessert and extras to share with a neighbor, babysitter or anyone else who would love to know you're thinking of them.

BUSY-DAY MAINS

Chicken in Mushroom Gravy
Irene Robinson
Cincinnati, OH

*A wonderful dish that cooks while you're away. Just add
a vegetable and a tossed salad to complete the meal.*

4 boneless, skinless
  chicken breasts
salt and pepper to taste
10-3/4 oz. can cream of
  mushroom soup

1/2 c. dry white wine or
  chicken broth
4-oz. can sliced mushrooms,
  drained
cooked rice or egg noodles

Season chicken breasts with salt and pepper; arrange in a 4-quart
crockpot. In a bowl, whisk together mushroom soup and wine or broth;
spoon over chicken. Add mushrooms. Cover and cook on low setting for
7 to 9 hours, or on high setting for 3 to 4 hours, until chicken is tender.
Serve chicken and gravy over cooked rice or noodles. Makes 4 servings.

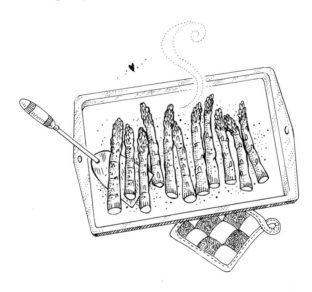

Pop an easy side of roast asparagus in the oven. Arrange
trimmed asparagus on an oiled baking sheet. Bake at
425 degrees for 10 to 15 minutes, until fork-tender and
golden. Sprinkle with finely shredded Parmesan cheese
and a drizzle of lemon juice. Delicious with broccoli, too.

CLASSIC CROCKPOT RECIPES

Mary's Meatloaf in a Crock
Marian Forck
Chamois, MO

My friend Mary made this one night when she had us over for supper. It is so good! Afterwards, we played rummy and had a good time together.

1-1/2 lbs. ground beef
8-oz. can tomato sauce, divided
2 eggs, beaten
2/3 c. dry bread crumbs

1/2 c. milk
2 T. onion, grated
1 t. salt

In a large bowl, combine uncooked beef, 1/4 cup tomato sauce and remaining ingredients. (Cover and refrigerate remaining tomato sauce.) Mix well and shape into a loaf to fit a 4-quart crockpot. Cover and cook on low setting for 5 to 6 hours, until meatloaf is cooked through. Warm remaining tomato sauce; spoon over meatloaf. Slice and serve. Makes 6 servings.

Dried, minced onions can be a real time-saver! If the recipe has a lot of liquid, such as soups and stews, it's easy to switch. Just substitute one tablespoon of dried onions for every 1/3 cup diced fresh onion.

BUSY-DAY MAINS

Mom's Cream Pork Chops
Beverly Moore
Lake Station, IN

My mom always made this, using her mother's recipe. The soup makes delicious gravy for mashed potatoes.

4 to 6 thick-cut pork chops
10-3/4 oz. can cream of
  chicken soup

1-1/4 c. water
salt, pepper and salt-based herb
  seasoning to taste

Layer pork chops in a 4-quart crockpot; set aside. Whisk together chicken soup, water and seasonings in a bowl; spoon over pork chops. Cover and cook on low setting for 7 to 8 hours, until pork chops are tender. Makes 4 to 6 servings.

Melt-in-Your-Mouth Pork Chops
Sasha Church
Broussard, LA

Make this a quick weeknight dinner by putting it in the crockpot in the morning. Serve with instant mashed potatoes and a bag of microwave steamed veggies! The pork chops will be very tender.

14-oz. can chicken broth
10-3/4 oz. can cream of
  chicken soup
1-oz. pkg. onion soup mix

1-oz. pkg. pork gravy mix
4 boneless or bone-in pork
  chops, 1/2-inch thick
1 t. garlic powder, or to taste

In a 4-quart oval crockpot, whisk together chicken broth, chicken soup, soup mix and gravy mix; set aside. (Any lumps will dissolve during cooking.) Lightly season pork chops on both sides with garlic powder. Layer pork chops in crock, pushing down to cover with soup mixture. Cover and cook on low setting for 6 to 8 hours. Serves 4.

Baked potatoes are an easy side with slow-cooked meats.
Scrub, pierce and bake potatoes at 350 degrees for 60 minutes,
turning once, or until fork-tender.

Spicy BBQ Pork Chops

Faith Srader
Hutchinson, KS

I came up with this recipe when I wanted something different from the usual barbecue pork chops, that I could just put in crockpot and forget about. The onion and green pepper are optional, but add flavor and color.

2 10-oz. cans diced tomatoes
    with green chiles, drained
1 c. spicy honey chipotle
    barbecue sauce
2 t. garlic powder

2 T. plus 1 t. oil, divided
1/2 c. onion, chopped
1/2 c. green pepper, chopped
4 thick-cut pork loin chops
salt and pepper to taste

In a large bowl, mix together tomatoes, barbecue sauce and garlic powder; set aside. Heat one teaspoon oil in a skillet over medium-high heat. Sauté onions and peppers until soft; add to tomato mixture. Heat remaining oil in same skillet over medium-high heat. Season pork chops with salt and pepper; add to skillet. Brown for about 3 minutes per side. Add 2 pork chops to a 5-quart crockpot; cover with half of tomato mixture. Repeat layering. Cover and cook on high setting for 4 hours, or on low setting for 6 hours, until pork chops are very tender. Makes 4 servings.

Crisp coleslaw is a must with barbecue! Blend a bag
of shredded coleslaw mix with 1/2 cup mayonnaise,
2 tablespoons milk, one tablespoon vinegar and
1/2 teaspoon sugar. Chill for one hour before serving.

BUSY-DAY MAINS

Slow-Simmered Ham & Beans
Debra Arch
Kewanee, IL

This recipe is so delicious and easy! Once everything is in the crockpot, you can go outside and enjoy the nice weather. Use a veggie chopper to chop the celery, onions and ham. It is less messy and faster than chopping by hand, and you can make the pieces as fine or as chunky as you like.

32-oz. pkg. dried Great Northern
    beans, rinsed and sorted
4 c. fresh water
4 stalks celery, finely chopped
3 to 4 onions, finely chopped

8-oz. pkg. cooked ham steak,
    finely chopped
1/2 t. salt
1 to 2 T. pepper, to taste

Add beans to a large container; cover generously with water. Cover and let soak overnight. In the morning, drain beans and rinse. Add beans to a 6-quart crockpot along with 4 cups fresh water. Add remaining ingredients; stir well. Cover and cook on high setting for 5 to 6 hours. Stir again and serve. Makes 8 servings.

Instead of soaking, dried beans can be slow-cooked overnight on low. Cover with water and add a teaspoon of baking soda. In the morning, just drain and proceed with the recipe.

Mom's Coffee Pot Roast

Maria McGovern
Stratford, NJ

This is so easy and delicious! My mom always served this in the fall and winter. It was so nice to come home from school and smell it cooking. Mom passed the recipe on to me 30 years ago, in a cookbook she made for me for my bridal shower. I've always made homemade biscuits to go along with this dinner...oh-so good!

2 to 3 lbs. stew beef cubes
4 potatoes, peeled and cut
   into chunks
8-oz. pkg. baby carrots

1 onion, cut into chunks
salt and pepper to taste
10-3/4 oz. can tomato soup
1 c. brewed coffee

Cut up any larger beef cubes, as desired. Combine beef and vegetables in a 6-quart crockpot; season with salt and pepper. Stir together tomato soup and coffee in a bowl; spoon over beef mixture. Cover and cook on low setting for 7 to 9 hours, until beef is tender. Makes 4 to 6 servings.

A family recipe book is a wonderful way to preserve one generation's traditions for the next. Ask everyone to share their most-requested recipes and arrange handwritten or typed recipes into a book. Have enough copies made for everyone...sure to be cherished!

BUSY-DAY MAINS

Bob's Chicken & Dumplings

Marian Forck
Chamois, MO

My brother Bob brought this to a potluck dinner for the family.
He ended up sharing the recipe with all his siblings!

4 boneless, skinless chicken
   breasts
1 onion, chopped
2 10-3/4 oz. cans cream of
   mushroom soup

2 T. butter, sliced
2 7-1/2 oz. tubes refrigerated
   biscuits, torn into pieces
1 to 2 T. all-purpose flour

Arrange chicken breasts in a greased 6-quart crockpot; top with
onion, soup and butter. Add enough water to cover chicken; stir gently.
Cover and cook on high setting for 5 to 6 hours, until chicken is tender.
Remove chicken; shred and stir into mixture in crock. About 30 minutes
before serving time, roll each biscuit piece in flour. Place biscuit pieces
on top; cover and continue cooking for 30 minutes, or until biscuits are
done. Serves 6 to 8.

Shirley's Salsa Beef

Shirley Howie
Foxboro, MA

Use your favorite salsa for this tasty dish, or try a new one! Add a
green salad and some buttered rolls to complete the meal.

1 T. oil
2 lbs. stew beef cubes
16-oz. jar favorite salsa
8-oz. can Italian-seasoned
   tomato sauce

1 c. canned diced tomatoes
2 T. brown sugar, packed
1 T. soy sauce
2 cloves garlic, minced
cooked rice

Heat oil in a large skillet over medium-high heat. Working in batches,
brown beef in oil; drain. Add browned beef to a 4-quart crockpot coated
with non-stick vegetable spray. Add remaining ingredients except rice;
stir well to combine. Cover and cook on low setting for 6 to 8 hours.
Serve over cooked rice. Makes 5 to 6 servings.

Dad's Homemade Spaghetti Sauce

Ed Kielar
Whitehouse, OH

A great recipe to make and pass down in your family. Serve over hot spaghetti or another favorite pasta...pass the Parmesan, please!

1 lb. ground beef	2 T. fresh parsley, minced
4 14-1/2 oz. cans diced tomatoes	2 T. garlic powder
6 6-oz. cans tomato paste	2 t. dried basil
1 c. beef broth	2 t. dried oregano
1/4 c. brown sugar, packed	1 t. salt

Cook beef in a skillet over medium heat until no longer pink. Drain; transfer to a 5-quart crockpot. Stir in tomatoes with juice and remaining ingredients. Cover and cook on low setting for 6 to 8 hours, until hot and bubbly. Serve as desired. Makes 10 to 12 servings.

Slow-cooked spaghetti sauce adds homemade flavor to so many meals. Bake it with penne pasta and mushrooms, spoon it over a meatloaf or just toss with spaghetti... you'll want to make plenty to freeze for later!

SIMPLY DELICIOUS MAINS

CLASSIC CROCKPOT RECIPES

Teriyaki Pork Roast

Paula Marchesi
Auburn, PA

Using a crockpot...yes! It's quick, easy and always delicious. I actually have four crockpots, and at times, I have three of them going at once. One for an appetizer, one for our main meal, and one for either a side or a dessert. It's so handy! When you have company, you have more time to spend with them, too.

3/4 c. unsweetened apple juice
2 T. sugar
2 T. soy sauce
1 T. vinegar
1 t. ground ginger
1/4 t. garlic powder

1/8 t. pepper
3-lb. boneless pork loin roast,
   cut in half
2-1/2 T. cornstarch
3 T. cold water

In a 5-quart crockpot, combine apple juice, sugar, soy sauce, vinegar and seasonings; mix well. Add roast; turn to coat. Cover and cook on low setting for 7 to 8 hours, until roast is tender. Remove roast to a platter; cover to keep warm. In a saucepan, combine cornstarch and cold water; cook and stir over low heat until smooth. Stir in juices from crockpot; bring to a boil. Cook and stir for 2 minutes, or until thickened. Slice roast; serve with sauce. Makes 8 servings.

Set up a framed menu at your next family gathering.
Everyone will be so happy to know that delicious
dishes like "Great-Grandmother's Pot Roast" and
"Aunt Betty's Pudding Cake" await!

SIMPLY DELICIOUS MAINS

Company Pork Roast

Kathryn Hinkle
Clinton, TN

*I make this easy recipe often. It is delicious served with
mashed potatoes and fresh green beans. So simple,
yet feels fancy enough for company!*

1 onion, sliced
2-1/2 to 3-lb. boneless pork
   loin roast
1 c. hot water
3 T. red wine vinegar
2 T. soy sauce

1 T. catsup
1/4 t. garlic powder
1/2 t. salt
1/2 t. pepper
Optional: 1/8 t. hot pepper sauce

Layer onion slices in a 5-quart crockpot; place roast on top and set
aside. Mix together remaining ingredients in a small bowl; spoon over
roast. Cover and cook on low setting for 6 to 8 hours, or on high setting
for 3 to 4 hours, until roast is tender. Remove roast to a platter; cover
and let stand for a few minutes. Slice roast; serve with drippings from
crock. Makes 8 servings.

Drizzle salad greens with a quick & easy honey dressing.
Whisk together 1/2 cup balsamic vinegar, 1/4 cup honey,
1/4 cup olive oil and one teaspoon soy sauce until smooth.
Top salad with ruby-red pomegranate seeds or dried
cranberries and a toss of candied pecans...yum!

CLASSIC CROCKPOT RECIPES

Cheesy Chicken Spaghetti
Marsha Baker
Palm Harbor, FL

Simple and delicious...always a hit with young and old.
Get ready to be asked for this recipe!

16-oz. pkg. spaghetti, uncooked
16-oz. pkg. pasteurized process
    cheese, cubed
12-1/2 oz. can chicken breast,
    drained and flaked
10-3/4 oz. can cream of
    mushroom soup
10-3/4 oz. can cream of
    chicken soup

10-oz. can diced tomatoes with
    green chiles
4-oz. can mushroom stems &
    pieces, drained
1/2 c. onion, diced
Optional: 1/2 c. green pepper,
    diced
1/2 c. water
salt and pepper to taste

Cook spaghetti according to package directions, just until tender. Drain; add to a 6-quart crockpot coated with non-stick vegetable spray. Add remaining ingredients; stir to mix well. Cover and cook on low setting for 2 to 3 hours, until bubbly and cheese is melted. Stir again just before serving. Serves 10 to 12.

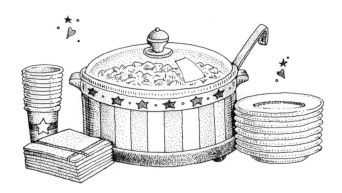

Crockpot recipes often make enough for sharing. Invite a neighbor or co-worker you've wanted to get to know better...encourage your kids to invite a friend. You'll be so glad you did!

SIMPLY DELICIOUS MAINS

Chicken Stew

Jeannie Stone
Nova Scotia, Canada

My family loves the taste of this chicken stew...it's a great way to get them to eat vegetables! It's good either with or without dumplings.

8 chicken breasts, thighs
    and/or drumsticks
1 c. buttermilk
2 t. garlic powder
6 to 7 potatoes, peeled and cubed
4 carrots, peeled and sliced

1 turnip, peeled and cubed
11-oz. can corn, drained
32-oz. container chicken broth
1.35-oz. pkg. onion soup mix
salt and pepper to taste

In a crockpot, combine chicken pieces, buttermilk and garlic powder; mix gently. Refrigerate for 2 hours or overnight. Add remaining ingredients to crockpot. Cover and cook on low setting for 5 to 6 hours, until chicken and vegetables are tender. If desired, once chicken is tender, drop dough for Dumplings by 1/4 cupfuls over stew. Cover and cook for one more hour. Uncover; let cool for 15 minutes and serve. Serves 4 to 6.

Dumplings:

1-3/4 c. all-purpose flour
2-1/2 t. baking powder
3/4 t. salt

1 t. pepper
1 c. whole or evaporated milk
1/4 c. butter, melted

Whisk together flour, baking powder, salt and pepper; stir in milk and butter.

137

Yankee Pot Roast

Beckie Apple
Grannis, AR

My grandmother "Mimie" handed down this pot roast recipe. Growing up in the South, we didn't have many recipes called "Yankee." But Mimie told me that because it has Polish sausage and celery in it, we'd call it a Yankee dish!

2-1/2 lb. beef chuck roast
1/2 t. seasoned salt
1/2 t. pepper
1-1/2 lbs. new redskin potatoes
1 lb. baby carrots
1 yellow onion, quartered

4 stalks celery, cut into 3 to
   4-inch pieces
1.35-oz. pkg. onion soup mix
1 lb. smoked Polish sausage, cut
   into 3-inch pieces

Sprinkle both sides of beef roast with seasoned salt and pepper; place roast in a 5-quart crockpot. Layer with potatoes, carrots, onion and celery; sprinkle soup mix over all. Place sausage on top. Cover and cook on low or medium setting for 5 to 7 hours, until beef and vegetables are tender. Remove roast to a platter; slice or shred. Surround with vegetables and sausage; serve. Makes 6 to 8 servings.

Serve delicious gravy with crockpot roasts! Ladle 2 cups of crockpot juices into a saucepan. Bring to a boil over medium-high heat. Combine 2 tablespoons cornstarch and 3 tablespoons water; whisk into the boiling liquid. Cook and stir for a few minutes, until gravy thickens. Season with salt and pepper and serve.

SIMPLY DELICIOUS MAINS

Spaghetti for Sharing

Sharon Theisen
Saint Cloud, MN

Friends love the taste of this spaghetti! It's a favorite easy meal served with a crisp tossed salad and garlic toast.

1 lb. ground beef	1/2 t. garlic powder
3 c. tomato juice	1/2 t. dry mustard
8-oz. can tomato sauce	1/4 t. allspice
4-oz. can sliced mushrooms,	1/4 t. pepper
drained	4 oz. spaghetti, uncooked and
1 T. garlic, minced	broken into 4-inch pieces

Brown beef in a skillet over medium heat; drain and add to a 4-quart crockpot. Add remaining ingredients except spaghetti; stir. Cover and cook on low setting for 6 to 7 hours, or on high setting for 3 to 3-1/2 hours. During last hour, turn to high setting; stir in spaghetti. Cover and continue cooking until spaghetti is tender. Makes 6 servings.

Shells & Cheese with Bacon

Jennifer Levy
Warners, NY

I love to make macaroni & cheese for company, but it can be a lot of work when I just want to visit with my guests. This recipe is the perfect solution! It cooks to creamy, cheesy perfection while I am free to mingle with my houseful of family & friends.

16-oz. pkg. medium pasta shells,	5-oz. can evaporated milk
uncooked	2 c. 2% milk
1/2 c. butter, diced	10-3/4 oz. can Cheddar cheese
Optional: 1/8 t. pepper	soup
16-oz. pkg. shredded Cheddar	5 slices bacon, crisply cooked
cheese, divided	and crumbled
2 eggs, beaten	

Cook pasta according to package directions, just until tender. Drain; add to a 6-quart crockpot. Add butter; stir until melted. Add pepper, if using. Stir in 2 cups shredded cheese. In a bowl, combine eggs, milks and cheese soup; whisk until smooth and stir into pasta. Stir in bacon; sprinkle with remaining cheese. Cover and cook on low setting for 3 to 5 hours, until hot and bubbly. Serves 8.

CLASSIC CROCKPOT RECIPES

Cabbage, Potato & Sausage Stew

Judi Towner
West End, NC

A hearty and very flavorful meal for a cold night's supper. You can use any favorite smoked sausage that you like. Serve with crusty buttered bread to sop up the tasty juices.

1/2 head cabbage, cut
  into chunks
1 lb. Kielbasa sausage, cut into
  1/2-inch slices
6 Yukon Gold potatoes, quartered
1 yellow onion, sliced

salt and pepper to taste
1/2 c. chicken broth
6 T. butter, melted
1/4 c. water
1 T. garlic, minced

Layer cabbage, sausage, potatoes and onion in a 5-quart crockpot. Season with salt and pepper; set aside. In a bowl, whisk together remaining ingredients; spoon over top. Cover and cook on high setting for 3-1/2 hours, or until potatoes are fork-tender. Makes 6 servings.

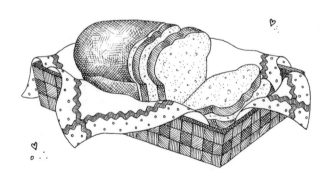

Whip up a loaf of beer bread for dinner. Combine 2 cups self-rising flour, 3 tablespoons sugar and a 12-ounce can of beer in a greased loaf pan. Bake at 350 degrees for 25 minutes, then drizzle with melted butter.
Warm and tasty!

SIMPLY DELICIOUS MAINS

Balsamic Chicken

Rebecca Johnson
Alpine, CA

This recipe is a family favorite and comes together quickly!
We enjoy it served with a tossed green salad and fresh bread.

4 boneless, skinless chicken
   breasts
3/4 c. balsamic vinegar
1 T. extra-virgin olive oil
4 cloves garlic, minced

1 T. onion, minced
2 t. dried basil
1 t. salt
1 t. pepper

Arrange chicken breasts in a 5-quart crockpot; set aside. Combine remaining ingredients in a small bowl; spoon over chicken. Cover and cook on low setting for 6 hours, or until chicken is cooked through. Makes 4 servings.

Tina's BBQ Chicken

Tina Goodpasture
Meadowview, VA

Chicken has always been my favorite meat. This is why I love this recipe. Your house will smell like heaven while it is cooking and your mouth will water. It's quick to toss together, too...you've gotta try it!

4 to 6 boneless, skinless
   chicken breasts
18-oz. bottle favorite barbecue
   sauce

1/4 c. vinegar
1/4 c. brown sugar, packed
1 t. garlic powder
Optional 1 t. red pepper flakes

Arrange chicken in a 5-quart crockpot; set aside. Mix remaining ingredients in a bowl; spoon over chicken. Cover and cook on low setting for 4 to 6 hours, until chicken is tender and juices run clear when pierced. Serves 4 to 6.

Hosting a dinner party? Stick to simple tried & true recipes you know will turn out well. You'll be happy and so will your guests.

CLASSIC CROCKPOT RECIPES

Pepper Steak

Sara Huntley
Dodge Center, MN

Better and faster than take-out! I can't count how many times I've made this dish over the years. Serve over cooked rice or noodles, or with mashed or baked potatoes...it's good any way you serve it.

2 lbs. beef sirloin steak,
   cut into strips
3/4 c. beef broth, heated
3 cubes beef bouillon
1/4 c. soy sauce
2 t. Worcestershire sauce
2 T. honey
1 t. ground ginger

1/2 t. salt
1/2 t. pepper
2 T. cornstarch
3 red, orange and/or yellow
   peppers, thickly sliced
1 c. onion, sliced
3 cloves garlic, minced

Add beef strips to a 4-quart crockpot; set aside. In a bowl, combine hot beef broth, bouillon cubes, sauces, honey, seasonings and cornstarch. Stir well, crushing the bouillon cubes; spoon over beef. Add peppers, onion and garlic on top of beef. Cover and cook on low setting for 6 hours, or on high setting for 3 hours, until beef and peppers are tender. If possible, stir halfway through cooking time. Stir again and transfer to a serving dish. Makes 6 servings.

Stem and seed a green pepper in a flash...hold the pepper upright on a cutting board. Use a sharp knife to slice each of the sides from the pepper. You'll then have 4 large seedless pieces, ready for slicing or chopping.

Beef Stroganoff

Beth Richter
Canby, MN

Beef Stroganoff is such a comforting and delicious meal. With a crockpot, you can make it any time of year without heating up your house. Serve over cooked noodles or rice, or over zucchini "zoodles" or riced cauliflower for a healthy alternative.

2-1/2 lbs. stew beef cubes
10-3/4 oz. can cream of
   mushroom soup
1.35-oz. pkg. onion soup mix
8-oz. pkg. sliced mushrooms
1/2 t. cornstarch

8-oz. pkg. cream cheese,
   softened
1 c. sour cream
salt and pepper to taste
Optional: snipped fresh parsley
   or thyme

Spray a 5-quart crockpot with non-stick spray. Add beef cubes, mushroom soup, soup mix and mushrooms; stir until combined. Cover and cook on low setting for 6 to 8 hours. About 30 minutes before serving, stir in cornstarch. Add cream cheese and allow to melt into beef mixture, stirring occasionally, until well blended. Stir in sour cream; season with salt and pepper. Serve over cooked egg noodles or rice; sprinkle with parsley or thyme, if desired. Makes 4 to 6 servings.

For a tasty change from regular pasta and rice, look for convenient frozen cauliflower "rice" and zucchini veggie spiral "noodles." Just cook according to package directions and serve.

CLASSIC CROCKPOT RECIPES

Irish Pork Stew

Shirley Howie
Foxboro, MA

When the weather turns cool here in New England, I like to try new recipes in my crockpot. After I made this stew for the first time, I knew I'd definitely be making it again! You could substitute beef for the pork, if you prefer. Either way, it will be very tasty!

1 lb. lean boneless pork, cut into
   1-inch cubes
1 T. oil
2-1/2 c. turnips, peeled and cut
   into 1/2-inch cubes
1-1/2 c. potatoes, peeled and cut
   into 1/2-inch cubes
1-1/2 c. carrots, peeled and cut
   into 1/2-inch cubes

2 onions, cut into wedges
1/4 c. quick-cooking tapioca,
   uncooked
1/4 t. dried thyme
1/2 t. salt
1/4 t. pepper
3 c. beef broth

In a large skillet over medium-high heat, brown pork in hot oil; drain. Meanwhile, in a 6-quart crockpot, stir together remaining ingredients except beef broth. Add browned pork and broth; stir well. Cover and cook on low setting for 8 to 10 hours, until pork and vegetables are tender. Stir again and serve. Makes 4 to 5 servings.

The better part of one's life
consists of one's friendships.
– Abraham Lincoln

SIMPLY DELICIOUS MAINS

Sunday Chicken

Vicky Lamb
Grantsville, UT

Everyone loves this dish! I love the fact that it cooks while I'm at church, and it's easily doubled. Served with a crisp salad, hot rolls and a yummy dessert, you've got a perfect meal to fellowship around. What are you waiting for? Turn on the crockpot and invite someone to share it. You'll be glad you did.

4 boneless, skinless chicken
   breasts, cubed
10-3/4 oz. can cream of
   chicken soup
1-oz. pkg. ranch salad
   dressing mix

1/4 c. water
1/2 c. cream cheese, softened
Optional: 4-oz. can sliced
   mushrooms, drained
8-oz. pkg. wide egg noodles,
   cooked

Place chicken breast cubes in a lightly greased 4-quart crockpot. Combine next 3 ingredients. Spoon over chicken. Cover and cook on low setting for 3 to 4 hours. Stir in cream cheese and mushrooms, if using. Gently stir cooked noodles into chicken mixture and serve. Makes 4 to 5 servings.

Try roasting veggies in the crockpot...so simple and delicious! Just drizzle with a couple tablespoons of olive oil and season to taste. Cook on high setting for about 3 hours, stirring occasionally.

CLASSIC CROCKPOT RECIPES

Company Beef Brisket
Sonja Rothstein
Pinehurst, NC

I keep the ingredients for this recipe on hand...it's so easy to put together. When family & friends enjoy this dish, they can't believe how tender and delicious it is. Served with a side of potatoes, or sandwich-style on hearty rolls, it simply can't be beat!

3-1/2 lb. beef brisket,
    fat trimmed
1-1/2 t. chili powder
3/4 t. garlic powder

1/2 t. onion powder
1/4 t. celery seed
1-1/2 t. salt
1/2 t. pepper

Pat brisket dry with paper towels; set aside. Combine remaining ingredients in a cup. Mix well and rub mixture over brisket, covering all sides. Place brisket in a 4-quart crockpot, cutting into 2 pieces if necessary to fit crock. Spoon half of Brisket Sauce over brisket; refrigerate remaining sauce. Cover and cook on high setting for 4 to 5 hours, until brisket is fork-tender. Remove brisket from crock; shred, if desired. Heat reserved sauce in microwave or on stovetop over low heat; serve over or alongside brisket. Serves 8.

Brisket Sauce:

1 c. catsup
1 c. chili sauce
1/2 c. brown sugar, packed
1/4 c. cider vinegar

1/4 c. Worcestershire sauce
1 t. dry mustard
Optional: 1 to 1-1/2 t. smoke-
    flavored cooking sauce

Combine all ingredients in a bowl; mix well.

Need a quick & easy side dish for Sunday dinner? Boil baby Yukon Gold potatoes whole... no need to cut or peel. Mash potatoes with milk, butter and ricotta cheese to taste. Scrumptious!

SIMPLY DELICIOUS MAINS

Turkey Breast with Gravy

Debbie Benzi
Binghamton, NY

This is an easy way to cook turkey, and you get delicious gravy as well! It's difficult to get really tasty gravy from a turkey breast as opposed to a whole turkey. I add the skin to the crockpot to give more flavor and depth to the drippings. Done this way, my gravy always comes out delicious! Relax and enjoy your holiday guests.

6 to 7-lb. turkey breast, thawed
   if frozen
1 T. butter
1 carrot, peeled and chopped
1 stalk celery, chopped
1 onion, chopped

6 cloves garlic, minced
7 T. all-purpose flour
2-1/2 c. chicken broth
1 t. dried thyme
salt and pepper to taste

Pull skin from turkey breast. Cut skin into 2 pieces and add to a skillet over medium heat (no need to add any butter or oil). Cook for 10 minutes, until browned and crisp. Transfer skin to a 6 to 7-quart crockpot; set aside. Add butter, vegetables and garlic to skillet. Cook for 10 minutes, stirring occasionally. Whisk in flour; cook for 2 minutes. Slowly whisk in chicken broth; bring to a boil. Stir in thyme; transfer gravy to crockpot. Season breast with salt and pepper; add to crockpot, meaty-side up. Cover and cook on low setting for 5 to 6 hours, until very tender and a meat thermometer inserted in center of breast reads 165 degrees. Remove breast to a platter; cover and let stand for 20 minutes before slicing. Pour gravy from crockpot through a strainer and serve with sliced turkey. Serves 8.

Not sure if the roast is done? Just check it with a meat thermometer. Recommended temperatures:

Chicken and turkey = 165 degrees
Beef and pork = 160 degrees for medium,
170 degrees for well-done

CLASSIC CROCKPOT RECIPES

Uncle Randy's Alfredo

Amanda Sandefur
Sarasota, FL

My brother-in-law and sister-in-law gave us this recipe after serving it on a family dinner night. It's so easy, cheesy and delicious!

3 boneless, skinless chicken
    breasts, cooked and shredded
2 14-1/2 oz. jars Alfredo sauce
1 c. water
1 T. garlic, minced
1 t. salt

1 t. pepper
3 c. shredded mozzarella cheese
1/2 c. grated Parmesan cheese
16-oz. pkg. penne pasta,
    uncooked
Garnish: snipped fresh parsley

In a large bowl, mix together chicken, Alfredo sauce, water, garlic, salt and pepper. Layer chicken mixture with cheeses in a 5-quart crockpot. Cover and cook on low setting for 2-1/2 to 3 hours, until bubbly and cheese is melted. Shortly before serving time, cook pasta according to package directions; drain. Serve chicken mixture over cooked pasta; garnish with parsley. Serves 6.

Broiled roma tomatoes make a tasty, quick garnish. Place tomato halves cut-side up on a broiler pan. Toss together equal amounts of Italian-seasoned dry bread crumbs and grated Parmesan cheese with a little oil. Spoon onto tomatoes and broil until golden.

SIMPLY DELICIOUS MAINS

Cheesy Tortellini

Amy Theisen
Sauk Rapids, MN

I use my homemade canned spaghetti sauce made from my homegrown tomatoes. But it's delicious with your favorite store-bought sauce, too. Serve with garlic bread...yum!

1/2 lb. regular or Italian ground
   pork sausage
1/2 lb. ground beef
24-oz. jar spaghetti sauce
14-1/2 oz. can diced tomatoes

1 c. sliced mushrooms
9-oz. pkg. frozen cheese tortellini
   or ravioli pasta, uncooked
1 c. shredded mozzarella cheese

In a skillet over medium heat, brown sausage and beef. Drain and transfer to a 5-quart crockpot. Stir in spaghetti sauce, tomatoes with juice and mushrooms. Cover and cook on low setting for 4 to 6 hours. Shortly before serving time, cook pasta according to package directions. Drain and stir into sausage mixture. Sprinkle with cheese; cover and cook for another 15 minutes, or until cheese is melted. Makes 6 to 8 servings.

Easy Herbed Chicken

Karen Smith
Rock Hill, SC

Scrumptious and so simple! I like to serve this chicken with potatoes and green beans from my garden.

4 bone-in chicken breasts
1 T. olive oil
1 t. paprika
1/2 t. dried thyme
1/2 t. dried basil
1/2 t. garlic powder

1/2 t. seasoned salt
1/2 t. pepper
1/2 t. browning & seasoning
   sauce
1/2 c. chicken broth

Remove skin from chicken breasts, if desired. In a small bowl, combine remaining ingredients except chicken broth; brush over chicken. Arrange chicken in a 4-quart crockpot; pour broth around chicken. Cover and cook on low setting for 4 to 5 hours, until chicken is very tender. Serves 4.

CLASSIC CROCKPOT RECIPES

My Chuck Roast Dinner

Glenna Banano
Cleveland, TX

I created this recipe myself after I discovered I didn't have all the ingredients for a recipe I had found online. My crockpot gave it the flavor I was looking for! My family enjoys warm cornbread with the roast and gravy.

3 to 4-lb. beef chuck roast
garlic powder, salt and pepper
    to taste
32-oz. container beef broth
1 yellow onion, cut into
    2-inch cubes
2 lbs. russet or Yukon Gold
    potatoes, peeled and cut into
    2-inch cubes

6 large carrots, peeled and cut
    into 2-inch pieces
3 stalks celery, cut into 2-inch
    pieces

Sprinkle roast generously on both sides with seasonings; place in a 6-quart crockpot. Pour beef broth around roast and place onion on top. Cover and cook on high setting for 4 hours. Remove lid; add potatoes, carrots and celery. Cover and cook for another one to 2 hours, until roast and vegetables are very tender. Remove roast to a platter. Slice or shred roast; serve with vegetables. Makes 4 to 6 servings.

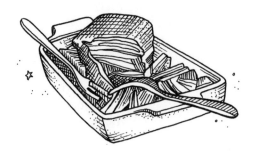

Slow-cook an extra-large roast for 2 tasty meals in one...
enjoy roast beef or pork the first night, then serve shredded
meat with barbecue sauce on buns another night.

Saint Patrick's Corned Beef & Cabbage

Carol Davis
Edmond, OK

It just isn't Saint Pat's Day without this dish!

4 potatoes, cut into 2-inch cubes
4 carrots, peeled and sliced
   1-inch thick
1 onion, cut into 6 wedges
2-1/2 to 3-lb. flat-cut corned beef
   brisket with seasoning packet

12-oz. can regular or non-
   alcoholic beer
1 cabbage, cut into 8 wedges

Spray a 6-quart crockpot with non-stick vegetable spray; add potatoes, carrots and onion. Top with brisket; sprinkle seasoning packet over brisket. Add beer and enough water to just cover brisket. Cover and cook on low setting for 8 to 10 hours, until brisket is tender. Remove brisket to a cutting board; cover to keep warm. Add cabbage and increase to high setting. Cover and cook another 30 to 35 minutes, until cabbage is tender. To serve, slice brisket across the grain and arrange on platter. Remove vegetables from crockpot with a slotted spoon and arrange around sliced brisket. Serves 8.

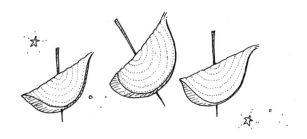

Insert wooden toothpicks into wedges of cabbage or onion...they'll hold together during slow cooking and can be served neatly. Discard picks before serving.

Mom's Sunday Chicken with Creamy Gravy

Victoria Mitchel
Gettyburg, PA

Slow-cooking chicken in this creamy gravy mixture produces the juiciest, most flavorful chicken! I came up with this recipe because I just love chicken with gravy, and also wanted the convenience of the crockpot. My husband couldn't stop eating it and kept saying how good it was. It's definitely a keeper at our house! We call it "Sunday Chicken" because it reminds us of old-fashioned Sunday dinners served after church. If you like lots of gravy (I do!), simply double the gravy part of the recipe.

3 lbs. boneless, skinless
   chicken breasts
salt and pepper to taste
Optional: 2 to 3 T. oil
6 T. butter
6 T. all-purpose flour
1 c. chicken broth
1 c. milk

2 T. white cooking wine or water
1/4 t. dried sage and/or poultry
   seasoning
1/2 t. salt
1/2 t. pepper
Optional: dried parsley to taste
mashed potatoes or cooked rice

Season chicken breasts with salt and pepper. If desired, brown chicken in oil in a large skillet over medium heat. Arrange chicken in a 6-quart crockpot sprayed with non-stick vegetable spray; set aside. Melt butter in a saucepan over medium heat. Stir in flour until thick and bubbly. Stir in chicken broth, milk and wine or water until smooth and sauce is thickened. Add sage or poultry seasoning, salt and pepper; stir well. Gently spoon sauce over chicken in crockpot. Sprinkle with parsley, if desired. Cover and cook on low setting for 7 to 8 hours, until chicken is very tender. Serve chicken and gravy with mashed potatoes or rice. Makes 6 to 8 servings.

Tie rolled cloth napkins with ribbon and slip a fresh sprig of sweet-scented thyme under the ribbon...charming!

SIMPLY DELICIOUS MAINS

Homespun Ham & Potatoes
Arlene Smulski
Lyons, IL

This creamy old oven favorite works beautifully in my crockpot while I'm away holiday shopping or busy wrapping gifts at home. When I'm finished with my busy chores, it is ready to serve. What a time-saver!

10-3/4 oz. can Cheddar
   cheese soup
1-1/2 c. whole milk
8 potatoes, peeled and
   thinly sliced
3 c. cooked ham, cubed

2 leeks, chopped
2-oz. jar sliced pimentos, drained
   and diced
1 t. paprika
1 t. pepper

In a large bowl, whisk together cheese soup and milk; set aside. In a greased 6-quart crockpot, layer half each of potatoes, ham, leeks, pimentos and soup mixture. Repeat layering; sprinkle with paprika and pepper. Cover and cook on low setting for 6 hours, or until potatoes are tender. Makes 8 servings.

Leeks are delicious in recipes, but may be sandy when purchased. To quickly clean leeks, slice them into 2-inch lengths and soak in a bowl of cold water. Swish them in the water and drain. Refill the bowl and swish again until the water is clear. Drain and pat dry...ready to use.

153

CLASSIC CROCKPOT RECIPES

Ginger Beef & Bok Choy

Carrie O'Shea
Marina del Rey, CA

Better than going for take-out!

2 T. peanut oil
1-1/2 lbs. boneless beef chuck
   roast, cut into 1-inch cubes
3 green onions, cut into
   1/2-inch pieces
6 cloves garlic, chopped
1 c. chicken broth
1/2 c. water

1/4 c. soy sauce
2 t. ground ginger
Optional: 1 t. Asian chili paste
9-oz. pkg. vermicelli pasta,
   uncooked
3 c. fresh bok choy, cut into
   1-inch pieces

Heat oil in a large skillet over medium-high heat. Working in batches, brown beef on all sides. Add onions and garlic to last batch of beef. Transfer beef mixture to a 6-quart crockpot. Add chicken broth, water, soy sauce, ginger and chili paste, if using; stir well. Cover and cook on low setting for 7 to 8 hours, until beef is tender. Shortly before serving, turn crockpot to high setting. Add pasta to crockpot and stir well. Add bok choy and stir again. Cover and cook on high setting for 15 minutes, or until pasta is tender and bok choy is tender-crisp. Makes 6 to 8 servings.

For a tasty change from rice, serve Asian-inspired dishes over rice noodles or thin spaghetti, or a bed of no-cooking-needed crispy chow mein noodles.

154

SIMPLY DELICIOUS MAINS

Pineapple Chicken

LaDeana Cooper
Batavia, OH

A great sweet-and-sour recipe! Serve over your favorite steamed rice...delicious.

1 to 2 T. oil
4 chicken thighs
2 8-oz. cans pineapple
  chunks, drained
3/4 c. yellow onion, diced
  and divided
1/2 c. brown sugar, packed
1/4 c. barbecue sauce
1/4 c. catsup

3 T. honey
2 T. soy sauce
1 T. ground ginger
2 cloves garlic, minced
1 T. cornstarch
1 T. water
1 green pepper, cut into strips
1 red pepper, cut into strips

Heat oil in a large skillet over medium heat. Add chicken and cook for about 2 to 3 minutes per side, until golden. Add pineapple and half of onion to a 5-quart crockpot; set aside. In a bowl, mix remaining ingredients except cornstarch, water, peppers and remaining onion. Add to crockpot; stir well. Arrange chicken skin-side up in crockpot over mixture. Cover and cook on low setting for 5 hours, or until chicken is nearly tender. Combine cornstarch and water in a cup; add to crock. Stir in peppers and remaining onion. Cover and cook an additional 30 minutes. Makes 4 servings.

Keep a small canning jar on hand for mixing up cornstarch and water for thickening crockpot dishes. Just combine them in jar, add lid and shake until cornstarch is dissolved.

CLASSIC CROCKPOT RECIPES

Sunday Chicken Cacciatore

Cindy Slawski
Medford Lakes, NJ

This recipe is great for a prep & forget about it kind of day. We love it in the fall and winter, as it really sticks to your ribs. It tastes even better the next day! Serve it over pasta, or as is.

4 boneless, skinless
   chicken breasts
28-oz. jar spaghetti sauce
6-oz. can tomato paste
4-oz. can sliced mushrooms,
   drained
1/2 yellow onion, minced

1/2 green pepper, diced
2 to 3 T. garlic, minced
1-1/2 t. dried oregano
1/2 t. dried basil
1/2 t. pepper
Optional: 1/4 t. red pepper flakes,
   1/8 t. garlic powder

Place chicken in a 5-quart crockpot. Stir in remaining ingredients. Cover and cook on low setting for 6 to 8 hours, until chicken is tender and cooked through. Makes 4 to 6 servings.

Stick o' Butter Entree

Lisa Staib
Tumbling Shoals, AR

My speedy dinner weapon...a crockpot, a stick of butter and a roast. Yummy...a juicy dinner couldn't be easier! We love this beef sliced and served with potatoes, beans or pasta, or shredded in a sandwich. This recipe can also be made using 2 to 4 pounds of boneless chicken breasts.

14-oz. can beef or chicken broth
2 to 4-lb. beef chuck roast
1 T. onion or garlic salt
salt and pepper to taste

1 stick butter, unwrapped
1 to 2 c. onions, peppers and/or
   mushrooms, chopped
   or sliced

Pour broth into a 5-quart crockpot. Sprinkle roast with seasonings and add to crockpot. Place whole stick of butter on top of roast. Cover and cook on low setting for 6 to 8 hours, or on high setting for 3 to 4 hours, until roast is tender. Add vegetables in the last hour, if desired. Slice roast and serve with juices from crock on the side. Makes 3 to 6 servings.

Beef & Sausage Meatballs & Spaghetti

Joyceann Dreibelbis
Wooster, OH

A tasty, family-pleasing crockpot recipe that doesn't take a lot of effort. Give it a try...this is sure to become a new favorite!

28-oz. can crushed tomatoes
2 T. tomato paste
1 t. dried oregano, divided
1 c. onion, finely chopped
3 sprigs fresh basil
4 cloves garlic, finely chopped
    and divided
1/4 c. grated Parmesan cheese

2 T. panko bread crumbs
1/2 lb. sweet Italian pork
    sausages, casings removed
1/2 lb. 90% lean ground beef
12-oz. pkg. spaghetti, uncooked
Optional: additional Parmesan
    cheese, fresh basil

In a 6-quart crockpot, whisk together tomatoes with juice, tomato paste and 1/2 teaspoon oregano. Stir in onion, basil and half of garlic; set aside. In a large bowl, combine Parmesan cheese, panko crumbs, remaining oregano and garlic. Add sausage and beef; mix gently. Shape into 20 balls, about 1-1/2 inches each; arrange on top of tomato mixture. Cover and cook on high setting for 4 to 5 hours, or on low setting for 6 to 7 hours, until meatballs are cooked through. About 20 minutes before serving, cook spaghetti according to package directions; drain. Toss spaghetti with sauce and meatballs. Serve with additional Parmesan cheese and basil, if desired. Serves 4 to 5.

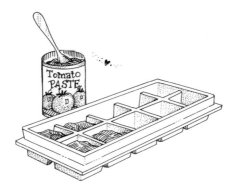

If a recipe calls for just a partial can of tomato paste, spoon the rest into ice cube trays and freeze for later use.

CLASSIC CROCKPOT RECIPES

Marian's Jambalaya

Marian Forck
Chamois, MO

We love jambalaya and this is so good. It is something that we only fix for special occasions. I've always liked making this dish and everyone wants to have some to take home. I am not a big fan of shrimp, so I leave it out...it's still delicious with the chicken and sausage.

2 lbs. boneless, skinless chicken breasts, cut into chunks
1 lb. smoked pork sausage, cut into chunks
28-oz. can diced tomatoes
1 c. onion, chopped
1 c. green pepper, chopped
3 stalks celery, chopped
2 c. chicken broth

2 to 3 T. garlic, minced
1 T. Cajun or Creole seasoning
1 t. dried thyme
1 t. dried oregano
1 lb. medium shrimp, peeled and cleaned
1-3/4 c. long-cooking rice, uncooked

Combine all ingredients except shrimp and rice in a 5-quart crockpot. Mix gently. Cover and cook on medium or low setting for 5 hours, until chicken and sausage are nearly cooked though. Stir in shrimp and rice. Increase to high setting; cover and cook another 30 minutes. Mix again and serve. Serves 6 to 8.

Wide-rimmed soup plates are perfect for serving all kinds of saucy dishes, as well as hearty dinner portions of soup. There's even room to balance a breadstick or roll on the rim.

Moroccan Chicken

Marcia Marcoux
Charlton, MA

*A favorite from a family member! I like to use boneless,
skin-on chicken thighs...they cook up so tender.*

2 onions, halved and
   thinly sliced
4 carrots, peeled and sliced
3 lbs. chicken thighs and/or
   drumsticks
1/2 t. salt
1/2 c. golden raisins
1/2 c. dried apricots, coarsely
   chopped
14-oz. container chicken broth

1/4 c. tomato paste
2 T. all-purpose flour
2 T. lemon juice
2 cloves garlic, minced
1-1/2 t. ground cumin
1-1/2 t. ground ginger
1 t. cinnamon
3/4 t. pepper
Optional: toasted pine nuts,
   chopped fresh cilantro

Add onions and carrots to a 6-quart crockpot. Season chicken with
salt; add to crockpot. Top with raisins and apricots; set aside. In a bowl,
whisk together remaining ingredients except optional pine nuts and
cilantro. Spoon over chicken. Cover and cook on low setting for 6-1/2 to
7 hours, or on high setting for 3-1/2 to 4 hours, until chicken is tender.
Serve in bowls, sprinkled with pine nuts and cilantro, if desired. Makes
4 to 6 servings.

Host an adventure potluck! Ask each guest to bring
a favorite dish from "back home"...whether that's
somewhere across the USA or even around the world.

CLASSIC CROCKPOT RECIPES

Megan's Favorite Pork Roast
Heather Riley
Winterset, IA

Megan, our teenager, loves this pork roast and will even take the leftovers in her lunch to school. When I tell her I've got a roast in the crockpot for supper, she'll always ask, "Is it the one I like?"

5-lb. boneless double pork loin
   roast, tied with string
3/4 c. dry red wine or water
1/3 c. brown sugar, packed
1/4 c. vinegar
1/4 c. catsup
1/4 c. water

2 T. oil
1 T. soy sauce
2 cloves garlic, minced
1 t. curry powder
1/2 t. ground ginger
1/4 t. pepper
2 t. cornstarch

Place roast in a 6 to 7-quart crockpot; set aside. In a bowl, combine remaining ingredients except cornstarch. Mix well; spoon over roast. Cover and cook on low setting for 8 to 9 hours, until roast is tender. Remove roast to a platter; cover to keep warm. To make gravy, pour drippings from crock into a saucepan; stir in cornstarch. Bring to a boil over medium heat; cook and stir until thickened. Slice roast; serve with gravy. Makes 10 to 12 servings.

Thaw frozen roasts before slow cooking, if possible.
Otherwise, add a cup of water to the crock and cook on
high for the first hour; reduce to low and cook as usual.

SIMPLY DELICIOUS MAINS

Pork Roast & Sweet Potatoes

Anna McMaster
Portland, OR

A scrumptious meal for a chilly night.

3-lb. boneless pork roast
2 to 3 sweet potatoes, peeled
   and cubed
1 green or yellow pepper, cubed
1/2 c. apple cider

3 T. brown sugar, packed
1 t. cinnamon
salt and pepper to taste
Optional: 1 T. cornstarch,
   1 T. water

Place pork roast in a 5-quart crockpot. Top with sweet potatoes and pepper; set aside. In a bowl, mix together cider, brown sugar and seasonings; spoon over all. Cover and cook on high setting for 3-1/2 to 4 hours, or on low setting for 7 to 8 hours, until roast is tender. Remove roast to a platter. If desired, combine cornstarch and water; add to drippings in crock. Cover and cook for several minutes, until thickened. Slice roast; serve with vegetables and drippings. Makes 3 to 5 servings.

Hosting a festive holiday dinner? Let your crockpot help out by cooking up a scrumptious roast, or free up oven space by preparing a savory slow-cooked side dish. Crockpots are so handy, you may want more than one!

CLASSIC CROCKPOT RECIPES

Paula's Hungarian Cabbage

Marian Forck
Chamois, MO

*My sister-in-law Paula always makes unusual dishes, and we all love
to eat them at our big family gatherings. This is a good example!*

1 lb. ground hot Italian pork
  sausage
1 head cabbage, chopped into
  bite-size pieces
1 c. onion, chopped

29-oz. can tomato sauce
1/2 c. water
1/4 t. dried oregano
salt and pepper to taste

Brown sausage in a skillet over medium heat; drain. Transfer to a
5-quart crockpot; stir in remaining ingredients. Cover and cook on low
setting for 3 hours, or until cabbage is tender. Serves 6 to 8.

Honey-Mustard Sausage & Sauerkraut

Linda Peterson
Mason, MI

*This is a wonderful comfort-food recipe. It smells great while
it is cooking, and it tastes great too.*

3 to 4 carrots, peeled and cut
  into chunks
1 c. onion, thinly sliced
4 to 6 new redskin potatoes, each
  cut into 8 pieces
1 c. cabbage, chopped
14-oz. can sauerkraut

12-oz. pkg. smoked pork
  sausage, cut into chunks
1/2 c. low-sodium chicken broth
3 T. Dijon mustard
3 T. honey
1/4 t. pepper

In a 6-quart crockpot, layer carrots, onion, potatoes, cabbage, sauerkraut
and sausage; set aside. Whisk together remaining ingredients in a small
bowl; spoon over mixture in crock. Cover and cook on low setting for
6 to 8 hours, until vegetables are tender. Serves 5 to 6.

PARTY-TIME APPETIZERS

CLASSIC CROCKPOT RECIPES

Pulled Pork Nachos

Lisa Ashton
Aston, PA

These are really good! The slow-cooked pork adds some great flavor. You could also substitute beef, if you like.

3 to 4-lb. boneless pork
    shoulder, or 2 pork loins
12-oz. can root beer
15-oz. pkg. tortilla chips
8-oz. pkg. shredded Cheddar
    cheese

2 to 3 ripe tomatoes, chopped
4 green onions, chopped
3 jalapeño peppers, sliced
3.8-oz. can sliced black olives,
    drained
Garnish: sour cream

Place pork roast in a 5-quart crockpot; drizzle with root beer. Cover and cook on low setting for 7 to 8 hours, until very tender. Remove roast to a large bowl; cool slightly. Shred with 2 forks; do not drain juice, to keep it moist. At serving time, layer desired amount of tortilla chips on a large platter. Drain juice from pork and spread over chips. Layer with cheese, tomatoes, onions, peppers and olives. Dollop sour cream over nachos by heaping tablespoonfuls and serve. Makes 10 to 12 servings.

Make it easy for guests to mingle and chat...set up food at several tables, instead of one big party buffet. Place hot foods on one table, chilled foods at another, sweets at yet another. Your party is sure to be a success!

PARTY-TIME APPETIZERS

Cheesy Sausage Dip

Sandy Ann Ward
Anderson, IN

*It's always a special time when family & friends gather.
Laughter is shared, memories are made, and times are always
better shared with food like this easy, yummy dip.*

1 lb. ground pork sausage,
  browned and drained
3 8-oz. pkgs. cream cheese,
  cubed and softened

14-1/2 oz. can diced tomatoes
  with green chiles
Optional: 14-oz. jar pico de gallo
scoop-type tortilla chips

Add browned sausage to a 4-quart crockpot. Stir in cream cheese,
tomatoes with juice and pico de gallo, if desired. Cover and cook on low
setting for one to 2 hours, until cheese is melted, stirring occasionally.
Serve warm with tortilla chips. Makes 8 to 10 servings.

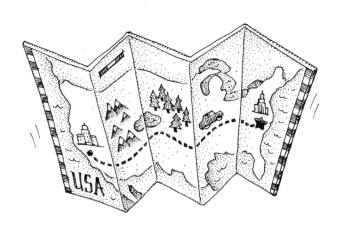

Paper fold-out maps make fun table coverings! Pick them up
for a song at a thrift store or used book store...cover with
a clear plastic tablecloth, if you like.

Hot Pimento Cheese Dip

Karen Wilson
Defiance, OH

The original recipe called for baking this dip, but I decided to use a crockpot so it would stay warm for a party. It's delicious and super-easy to make.

8-oz. pkg. shredded sharp
  Cheddar cheese
8-oz. pkg. shredded Monterey
  Jack cheese
7-oz. jar diced pimentos, drained

1/2 c. mayonnaise
1/4 c. sour cream
1 t. Worcestershire sauce
1/2 t. pepper
pita chips or snack crackers

Combine all ingredients except chips or crackers in a bowl. Mix well and transfer to a 3-quart crockpot. Cover and cook on low setting for one to 2 hours, until cheese is melted. Stir well; serve warm with pita chips or crackers. Makes 8 to 10 servings.

Swap party specialties with a friend! For example, offer to trade a crock of your super-secret-recipe chili for your best girlfriend's very best cheese dip. It's a super way to save party-planning time and money.

PARTY-TIME APPETIZERS

Momma's Meatballs

Kristy Wells
Ocala, FL

Whenever I make these meatballs for gatherings, they're very popular...I get many requests for the recipe! This is something I make often for dinner in fall and winter, serving it with mashed potatoes and a veggie. It makes a great potluck dish and keeps well as an appetizer, too. I hope you like it as much as we do!

24-oz. pkg. frozen cooked
   meatballs
18-oz. jar orange marmalade

2 T. Worcestershire sauce
1 T. Greek seasoning.
salt and pepper to taste

Combine all ingredients in a 4-quart crockpot; mix gently. Cover and cook on high setting for about 3 hours, until hot and bubbly. Turn to low setting for serving. Serves 8 to 10.

Invite friends over for snacks on game day. With hearty appetizers simmering in a crockpot or two, you'll be able to relax and enjoy the big game with your guests.

Thai-Style Chicken Wings
Thomas Campbell
Brooklyn Center, MN

These wings were created by mistake, but became a hit. I thought I had Thai wing sauce on hand, discovered I did not. I remembered my mom using peanut butter & jelly to make a barbecue sauce. I use a little more peanut butter, making it more of a Thai peanut sauce. I do not add salt because most peanut butter has a lot. If using low-sodium peanut butter, you can add a pinch to taste.

2 lbs. chicken wings, separated
Optional: 1 c. chicken broth
   or water
1/2 c. onion, thinly sliced
2-1/2 c. crunchy peanut butter

3 c. grape jelly
1/4 t. pepper
Optional: thinly sliced green
   onions

Place chicken wings in a 4-quart crockpot; add chicken broth or water if wings are frozen. Place onion on top of chicken wings; spoon peanut butter and jelly over all. Cover and cook on high setting for 4 to 6 hours, checking and stirring after 3 hours as needed, or on low setting for 6 to 8 hours. Remove wings to a platter; sprinkle with green onions, if desired. Serves 6 to 8.

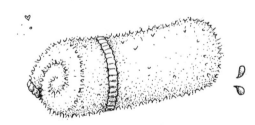

Serving yummy-but-sticky finger foods? Set a mini crockpot on low setting and fill with rolled-up, dampened fingertip towels. Guests will appreciate your thoughtfulness!

PARTY-TIME APPETIZERS

Teriyaki Meatballs

Chad Rutan
Gooseberry Patch

A favorite at tailgate parties.

1-1/2 c. cold water
3 T. cornstarch
1/2 c. sugar
1/2 c. soy sauce
1/4 c. honey
1 t. garlic powder

1 t. toasted sesame oil
3 14-oz. pkgs. frozen cooked
   meatballs
Garnish: sliced green onions,
   sesame seed

In a saucepan over medium heat, whisk together cold water and cornstarch. Stir in sugar, soy sauce, honey, garlic powder and sesame oil. Bring to a boil, stirring often. Boil for 2 minutes, or until thickened. Remove from heat. Add meatballs to a 5-quart crockpot; spoon sauce over meatballs. Cover and cook on high setting for 3 to 3-1/2 hours, stirring gently after 2 hours. Stir again; arrange meatballs on a platter and garnish as desired. Serves 8 to 10.

Aloha Sausages

Constance Lewis
Florence, AL

Love these sweet-and-sour little morsels! We found some pineapple party picks to use that were just perfect.

14-oz. pkg. cocktail sausages
15-1/4 oz. can crushed
   pineapple, drained

18-oz. jar peach preserves
8-oz. jar mustard

Combine all ingredients in a 4-quart crockpot. Cover and cook on high heat for 2 hours, or until hot and bubbly. Serves 8.

Set out a small discard dish for used toothpicks, to keep things tidy. Add one or 2 picks in the dish so guests will get the idea!

Copycat Mexican Spinach Dip

Jill Williams
Riley, KS

A Mexican restaurant favorite of mine. The restaurant is over an hour away, so I found a way to make my own "espinaca de queso" dip. I use one can of tomatoes with mild chiles and one original, but it can be made as hot as you like. For even more heat, add some chopped jalapeño peppers.

16-oz. pkg. regular or queso blanco pasteurized process cheese, cubed
2 8-oz. pkgs. cream cheese, cubed
2 14-1/2 oz. cans diced tomatoes with green chiles
1-1/2 c. spinach, chopped, thawed if frozen

1 c. whipping cream
1/2 c. onion, chopped
4 cubes chicken bouillon
Optional: 1/2 c. milk, or as needed
tortilla chips

Combine all ingredients except tortilla chips in a 6-quart crockpot. Cover and cook on low setting for 2 hours, or until cheese is melted. If a thinner consistency is desired, stir in optional milk as needed. Serve warm with tortilla chips. Makes 16 servings.

Partying outdoors? Keep bugs away from cool picnic beverages. Simply poke a hole through a paper cupcake liner, add a straw, flip it upside-down and use it as a beverage cap.

PARTY-TIME APPETIZERS

Spinach & Artichoke Dip

LaDeana Cooper
Batavia, OH

A favorite for my family around the holidays or for any get-together.

9-oz. pkg. frozen chopped spinach, thawed, drained and squeezed dry
14-oz. can artichoke hearts, drained and chopped
1 c. shredded Swiss cheese

1 c. jarred Alfredo sauce
1/2 c. mayonnaise
3/4 t. garlic salt
1/4 t. pepper
potato or tortilla chips

Mix all ingredients except chips in a 2-quart crockpot. Cover and cook for 2 to 4 hours, until bubbly and cheese is melted. Serve warm with your favorite chips. Makes 6 or more servings.

Chili Cheese Dip

Stacy Myers
Clear Spring, MD

This dip has been a favorite for every party we have. My friends are always asking me to bring it to their parties, too.

2 8-oz. pkgs. cream cheese, cubed and softened
15-1/2 oz. can chili, with or without beans
8-oz. pkg. shredded Cheddar cheese

8-oz. pkg. shredded mozzarella cheese
2 to 4 green onion tops, sliced, to taste
tortilla chips

Combine all ingredients except chips in a 4-quart crockpot in the order listed. Cover and cook on high setting for about one hour, stirring occasionally, until cheese is melted. Mix well; turn to low setting to keep warm. Serve warm with tortilla chips. Makes 10 servings.

Cut slices of crunchy carrot, zucchini and radish into fun shapes with mini cookie cutters...a great way to dress up an appetizer tray!

Fiesta Snack Mix

Rhonda Reeder
Ellicott City, MD

Crunchy, delicious and a little different from the usual snack mix! My teenage sons and their pals especially enjoy this. Sometimes I'll add a handful of roasted pepitas or peanuts for extra crunch.

4 c. bite-size crispy corn cereal	1/4 c. butter, melted
2 c. bite-size crispy wheat cereal	4 t. ranch salad dressing mix
4 c. mini pretzel twists or sticks	2 t. taco seasoning mix
2 c. bite-size corn chips	

In a 4-quart crockpot, combine cereals, pretzels and corn chips. Toss to mix and set aside. In a small bowl, whisk together remaining ingredients until well blended. Spoon over cereal mixture; stir to coat evenly. Cook, uncovered, on high setting for 2 hours, stirring every 20 minutes. Spread mixture on a large rimmed baking sheet; let cool for several minutes before serving. Store in a covered container. Makes 12 cups.

Silicone baking cups come in lots of fun colors. They're great for serving individual portions of party mix, and best of all, they're reusable.

PARTY-TIME APPETIZERS

Shelley's Salsa Dip

Monica Britt
Fairdale, WV

My sweet cousin Shelley gave me this scrumptious recipe.
My family loves it anytime, but especially as a snack
when watching football games on television.

1 lb. ground beef	16-oz. pkg. pasteurized process
1 lb. ground pork sausage	cheese, cubed
10-3/4 oz. can cream of	8-oz. jar favorite salsa
mushroom soup	scoop-type tortilla chips

Brown beef and sausage in a large skillet over medium heat. Drain well; transfer to a 5-quart crockpot. Add remaining ingredients except tortilla chips; mix well. Cover and cook on low setting for 2 hours, or until cheese is melted. Stir again; serve warm with tortilla chips. Serves 20.

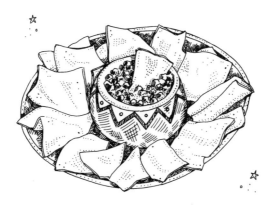

Enjoy the little things, for one day you may look back
and realize they were the big things.
– Robert Brault

CLASSIC CROCKPOT RECIPES

Sticky Chicken Bites

Ashley Hull
Gooseberry Patch

Everyone loves these yummy chicken morsels...
you might need to make a double batch!

3 boneless, skinless chicken
    breasts, cubed
1/2 c. low-sodium chicken broth
3/4 c. honey
2 T. soy sauce
1/3 c. grated Parmesan cheese

4 cloves garlic, minced
1 t. garlic powder
1/2 t. pepper
2 T. cold water
2 T. cornstarch

Add chicken cubes to a 4-quart crockpot; set aside. In a small bowl, combine remaining ingredients except water and cornstarch; mix well. Spoon over chicken; mix gently to coat. (If chicken isn't completely covered, stir in a little more broth or water.) Cover and cook on low setting for 2 hours, or until chicken is cooked through. In a cup, combine water and cornstarch; mix until cornstarch is dissolved. Drizzle evenly over chicken in crock. Increase setting to high; cover and cook for 30 minutes, or until sauce is thickened. Serves 8 to 10.

A basket brimming with colorful fresh vegetables
makes an easy and appealing centerpiece.

PARTY-TIME APPETIZERS

Stroganoff Meatballs
Thomas Campbell
Brooklyn Park, MN

I love making Beef Stroganoff, but don't always have time. Thus, this twist on stroganoff that's easy to make. I serve mine with toothpicks as an appetizer, or cook some egg noodles for a meal.

32-oz. pkg. frozen cooked
  meatballs
1 onion, diced
10-3/4 oz. can cream of
  mushroom soup

10-3/4 oz. can cream of
  chicken soup
1 c. sour cream
1 c. favorite Burgundy wine or
  beef broth

Place frozen meatballs in a 5-quart crockpot; add remaining ingredients and mix well. Cover and cook on low setting for 4 to 6 hours, stirring after 4 hours. Cook until meatballs are tender and sauce is creamy when stirred. Makes 6 to 8 servings.

Cheesy Chicken-Ranch Dip
Ildika Colley
Elkton, KY

So easy to make...so easy to eat! Mini sweet peppers cut in half are perfect for dipping.

2 8-oz. pkgs. reduced-fat cream
  cheese, cubed
8-oz. pkg. shredded Cheddar or
  mozzarella cheese
3/4 c. hot pepper sauce

1/2 c. ranch salad dressing
3 c. cooked chicken breast, diced
tortilla chips, crackers or
  cut-up vegetables

Combine cheeses, hot sauce and ranch dressing in a 4-quart crockpot. Cover and cook on low setting for one to 1-1/2 hours, until cheeses are melted, stirring often. Stir in chicken; cover and continue cooking for about 30 minutes, until heated through. Serve warm with chips, crackers or vegetables. Makes 8 servings.

For stand-up parties, make it easy on guests
by serving foods that can be eaten in one or 2 bites.

CLASSIC CROCKPOT RECIPES

Beachside Crab Dip

Michelle Newlin
Portage, PA

This dip is so tasty, we have even enjoyed it as a meal with a loaf of good bread! Serve with French bread slices or tortilla chips.

8-oz. container lump crabmeat,
   drained and flaked
1/2 c. cream cheese, softened
1/4 c. sour cream
1/4 c. mayonnaise
2 T. green onion, minced

2 to 3 cloves garlic, minced
1 t. Worcestershire sauce
1 T. lemon juice
salt and cracked pepper to taste
1 c. shaved Parmesan cheese,
   divided

Mix all ingredients in a 3-quart crockpot, reserving 1/2 cup Parmesan cheese for topping. Cover and cook on high setting for 2 hours, or on low setting for 4 hours; mix again. Top with reserved Parmesan cheese; serve warm. Makes 6 to 8 servings.

Fill a relish plate with crunchy fresh cut-up veggies as a simple side dish for sandwiches. Serve with a creamy dressing for dipping...try a blend of tangy Greek yogurt and basil pesto sauce.

PARTY-TIME APPETIZERS

Honey-Garlic Steak Bites

Patricia Harris
Hendersonville, TN

My brother came to visit and really enjoyed this recipe. Serve it over cooked rice or egg noodles, or with party picks as an appetizer.

1 to 2 T. sesame oil
2 lbs. beef chuck or round steak,
    cut into bite-size chunks
1/2 c. soy sauce
1/2 c. catsup
1/2 c. honey
4 cloves garlic, finely chopped
1/2 t. dried oregano
Optional: 2 T. cornstarch,
    2 T. cold water
Garnish: sliced green onions,
    sesame seed

Heat oil in a skillet over medium-high heat. Add beef and brown on all sides; drain and transfer to a 4-quart crockpot. Combine soy sauce, catsup, honey, garlic and oregano in a cup; mix well and spoon over beef. Cover and cook on low setting for 4 to 6 hours, or on high setting for 2 to 3 hours, until beef is tender. If a thicker sauce is desired, dissolve cornstarch in water and stir into sauce; cover and cook until thickened. Garnish with onions and sesame seed, as desired. Serves 8.

Planning an appetizers-only event? You'll want to serve at least 5 different dishes...allow 2 to 3 servings per person for each dish.

CLASSIC CROCKPOT RECIPES

Deluxe Pizza Dip

Jill Ball
Highland, UT

*Who doesn't like pizza? But it isn't always the healthiest choice.
Here's the best of both...a pizza dip you can enjoy with all
your favorite fresh veggies. Yummy!*

14-oz. jar pizza sauce
1 c. sliced pepperoni, chopped
8 green onions, chopped
1/2 c. red pepper, chopped
2-1/4 oz. can sliced black
    olives, drained

1 c. shredded mozzarella cheese
8-oz. pkg. cream cheese,
    softened
assorted cut vegetables

In a 1-1/2 quart crockpot, mix pizza sauce, pepperoni, onions, red
pepper and olives. Cover and cook on low setting for 3 to 4 hours, until
hot and bubbly. Add cheeses and stir until melted. Serve warm with
vegetables for dipping. Makes 16 servings.

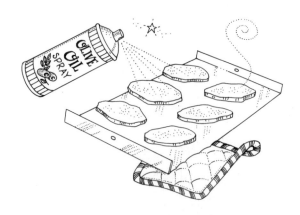

Hot dips are twice as tasty with homemade baguette crisps.
Thinly slice a French loaf and arrange slices on a baking sheet.
Sprinkle with olive oil and garlic powder. Bake at 400 degrees
for 12 to 15 minutes, until toasty.

PARTY-TIME APPETIZERS

White Pizza Dip

Mia Rossi
Charlotte, NC

Deliciously different! I like to sprinkle the dip with chopped fresh oregano to add a little color.

0.75-oz. pkg. garlic & herb salad dressing mix
16-oz. container sour cream
1 c. ricotta cheese
1/2 c. sliced pepperoni, chopped

1 c. shredded mozzarella cheese, divided
1 loaf Italian bread, sliced and cut into bite-size pieces

In a small bowl, combine salad dressing mix, sour cream, ricotta cheese, pepperoni and 3/4 cup mozzarella cheese. Spoon into a lightly greased 3-quart crockpot. Sprinkle reserved mozzarella cheese on top. Cover and cook on low setting for 2 to 3 hours, until bubbly and cheese is melted. Stir well; serve warm with bread pieces. Serves 6.

Warm Holiday Punch

Gladys Kielar
Whitehouse, OH

A warm beverage for special occasions that's sure to be enjoyed by everyone. Use additional cinnamon sticks as stirrers, if desired.

32-oz. bottle cranberry juice cocktail
32-oz. bottle pineapple juice

1/3 c. red-hot cinnamon candies
4-inch cinnamon stick

Combine all ingredients in a 3-quart crockpot. Cover and cook on low setting for 2 to 4 hours, until heated through and candies have melted. Discard cinnamon stick; serve warm. Makes 2 quarts.

Spoon creamy ranch dip into short plastic cups and add crunchy celery and carrot sticks. Nestle the cups in a tray of ice. Simple for guests to pick up and carry around!

Spiced Kielbasa Bites

Doreen Knapp
Stanfordville, NY

This is a great recipe to toss into the crockpot for tailgating and get-togethers in the backyard. Everyone enjoys the great warm spice flavors, but feel free to adjust the spice amounts. Serve with cocktail forks or party picks.

3/4 c. grape jelly
3/4 c. chili sauce
1/2 t. fresh ginger, peeled
   and grated
1/2 t. fresh nutmeg, grated
1/2 t. cinnamon

4 t. red wine
1-1/2 t. low-sodium soy sauce
1-1/2 t. mustard
12-oz. pkg. Kielbasa sausage,
   cut into 1-inch pieces

In a 3-quart crockpot, combine all ingredients except Kielbasa and stir well. Add Kielbasa; mix gently. Cover and cook on low setting for one to 2 hours, until heated through. Makes 6 servings.

A clear plastic over-the-door shoe organizer is super for pantry storage...just slip gravy mix packets, spice jars and other small items into the pockets.

PARTY-TIME APPETIZERS

Cranberry Sauerkraut Meatballs

Marsha Baker
Palm Harbor, FL

I have heard raves over this simple dish and it's very popular during the holidays. Guests tell me the sauerkraut puts it over the top. Try it...you'll like it!

15-oz. can whole-berry or
  jellied cranberry sauce
14-oz. can sauerkraut, drained
  and well rinsed

12-oz. bottle chili sauce
2/3 c. brown sugar, packed
32-oz. pkg. frozen cooked
  meatballs

In 4-quart crockpot, combine all ingredients except meatballs; mix well. Add meatballs; stir gently. Cover and cook on low setting for 3 to 4 hours, until hot and bubbly. Makes 12 to 15 servings.

Serve fizzy juice drinks in glasses with a bit of sparkle. Run a lemon wedge around the rims of glasses, then dip rims in superfine sugar. Garnish each with a sprig of fresh mint.

CLASSIC CROCKPOT RECIPES

Leona's Crunchy Party Mix
Leona Krivda
Belle Vernon, PA

This is easy to make if you have guests coming over...adults and children all like it! For the crispy cereal squares, I like to use a combination of corn, wheat and rice, but use what you prefer.

9 c. bite-size crispy cereal
  squares
1 c. doughnut-shaped oat cereal
2 c. mini pretzel twists,
  or pretzel pieces

1 c. cashews
6 T. butter, melted and hot
1 T. seasoned salt
1/4 c. Worcestershire sauce
1 t. garlic powder

Spray a 4-quart crockpot with non-stick vegetable spray. Add cereals, pretzels and cashews; toss to mix and set aside. Combine melted butter and salt in a bowl; stir until salt is dissolved. Stir in Worcestershire sauce and garlic powder; drizzle over cereal mixture. Toss for about 60 seconds to coat very well. Place a paper towel on top of crockpot to absorb any condensation. Cover and cook on low setting for 3 hours, stirring after one hour, after 2 hours and after 2-1/2 hours to avoid burning. Divide mixture among 2 to 3 parchment paper-lined baking sheets; spread evenly and let cool to room temperature. Serve immediately, or store in an airtight container for 2 to 3 weeks. Makes about 13 cups.

Need to chill lots of cans of soda quickly? Just add beverages to an ice-filled cooler along with enough water to cover them, plus a generous amount of salt. The salt will lower the temperature quickly, cooling the drinks, and you'll save valuable refrigerator space, too.

PARTY-TIME APPETIZERS

Jessica's Maple Mulled Cider

Julie Ann Perkins
Anderson, IN

This hot cider is great for trick-or-treating, Christmas caroling or simply sitting by the fire with a good book! We love going down the street to our Main Street fruit market to get fresh cider, apples and pumpkins. It is truly a wonderful, happy time! As an added bonus, this cider makes the whole house smell wonderful.

1/2 gal. cider	1 to 2 T. pure maple syrup
1 to 2 T. frozen orange juice concentrate	3 to 4 4-inch cinnamon sticks
	2 t. whole cloves

Combine all ingredients in a 3-quart crockpot; enclose spices in a spice bag, if desired. Stir well. Cover and cook on low setting for 2 hours, or until hot and bubbly. Discard spices; serve warm. Makes 8 servings.

Hosting a ladies' luncheon? Impress them with a yummy crockpot brie! Add a round of brie cheese to a crockpot and top with candied pecans and dried cranberries. Cover and cook on low setting for 4 hours, or until melted. Serve with sliced apples and slices of crusty bread. Yummy!

CLASSIC CROCKPOT RECIPES

Sonja's Sweet & Savory Bites

Sonja Rothstein
Pinehurst, NC

This recipe came to me when I was invited to a tailgate party and was asked to bring a dish. I had fun being creative with what I had on hand. Now I make this whenever I go to a tailgate or potluck...there are never any leftovers!

3 14-oz. pkgs. cocktail sausages, or 3 14-oz. pkgs. Kielbasa sausage, cut into 1-inch pieces

20-oz. can crushed pineapple in juice
12-oz. bottle chili sauce
1/2 c. brown sugar, packed

Place sausages in a 4-quart crockpot; set aside. In a bowl, mix undrained pineapple, chili sauce and brown sugar; spoon over sausages. Cover and cook on low setting for 2 to 3 hours, until bubbly and glazed. Serves 16.

Be sure to have extra copies on hand of that tried & true recipe everyone always raves about!

PARTY-TIME APPETIZERS

Kielbasa in a Crock

Leona Krivda
Belle Vernon, PA

I like quick & easy recipes and this is one of them. Put it all together and just let it simmer while you're waiting for your company.

2 lbs. Kielbasa sausage, cut into
   1-inch pieces
1 c. chunky applesauce

3/4 c. brown sugar, packed
2 T. Dijon mustard
2 cloves garlic, minced

Add Kielbasa to a 3-quart crockpot sprayed with non-stick vegetable spray; set aside. In a bowl, mix together remaining ingredients well; spoon over Kielbasa and stir to coat well. Cover and cook on high setting for 2 to 3 hours, until heated through. Makes 10 to 12 servings.

Maple-Apricot Kielbasa Bites

Judy Phelan
Macomb, IL

A great appetizer for football games.

16-oz. pkg. Kielbasa sausage,
   cut into 1-inch pieces
1 c. apricot preserves

1/2 c. pure maple syrup
2 T. apple juice

Combine all ingredients in a 3-quart crockpot. Cover and cook on low setting for 4 to 6 hours, until hot and bubbly. Serves 6 to 8.

Safety first! Keep hot foods hot, cold foods cold,
and don't leave anything at room temperature longer
than 2 hours, even if the food still looks just fine.

CLASSIC CROCKPOT RECIPES

Barb's Bean Dip

Barbara Klein
Newburgh, IN

My family loves this bean dip! It keeps them satisfied until dinner is ready. You can also serve this as a snack for an evening with friends.

16-oz. can refried beans
1 c. shredded Monterey
   Jack cheese
1 c. shredded Cheddar cheese
1 c. picante sauce
3/4 c. sour cream

3-oz. pkg. cream cheese,
   softened
1 T. chili powder
1/4 t. ground cumin
tortilla chips, salsa

Combine all ingredients except tortilla chips and salsa in a 1-1/2 quart crockpot. Mix well. Cover and cook on high setting for 2 hours, or until heated through, stirring once or twice. Serve warm with tortilla chips and salsa. Makes 4-1/2 cups.

Queso Dip

Rebecca Johnson
Alpine, CA

This dip is always a hit with our family and is a breeze to prepare! We like it with tortilla chips for dipping, or drizzled over a plate of tortilla chips and topped with diced green onions, sliced black olives, diced tomatoes, fresh cilantro and a dollop of sour cream. Excellent!

16-oz. pkg. pasteurized process
   cheese, cubed
10-oz. can diced tomatoes with
   green chiles

6 T. cream cheese, softened
1/2 t. ground cumin
Optional: 1 to 2 T. diced jalapeño
   peppers

Combine all ingredients in a 1-1/2 quart crockpot; stir well to combine. Cover and cook on low setting for 1-1/2 to 2 hours, until cheese is fully melted. Serve warm. Makes 8 servings.

Cheesy Hamburger Dip

Sandy Ann Ward
Anderson, IN

This tasty dip is a hit with everyone. Whether it's a gift wrapping party, cookie baking, gift exchange or game night for the family, it's a must. Santa even likes this on Christmas Eve!

3/4 of a 16-oz. pkg. pasteurized
    process cheese, cubed
10-3/4 oz. can cream of
    mushroom soup
10-3/4 oz. can tomato soup

1 lb. ground beef round
1/2 c. onion, chopped
1 green pepper, chopped
tortilla chips

Combine cheese cubes and soups in a 4-quart crockpot. Cover and cook on low setting for one to 2 hours, until cheese is melted. Meanwhile, brown beef with onion and pepper in a skillet over medium heat; drain. Add beef mixture to crock; stir well and heat through. Serve warm with tortilla chips. Serves 6 to 8.

Fill a big basket with festive paper napkins and plates... dollar store will do! When surprise guests pop in, you'll be all set to turn an ordinary dinner into a special occasion.

CLASSIC CROCKPOT RECIPES

Buffalo Ranch Wings

Tori Willis
Champaign, IL

Chicken wings are always the most popular item on our tailgating party buffet. Ranch dressing in the sauce makes these extra delicious! Sometimes I'll serve the wings with zucchini sticks for dipping, rather than the traditional celery sticks.

2 lbs. chicken wings, separated
1 c. buffalo wing sauce
1-oz. pkg. ranch salad
   dressing mix

salt and pepper to taste
Garnish: ranch salad dressing,
   sliced fresh chives,
   celery sticks

Arrange chicken wings in a 4-quart crockpot; set aside. In a large bowl, mix together wing sauce and salad dressing mix; season with salt and pepper. Spoon mixture over chicken wings; mix gently. Cover and cook on high setting for 2-1/2 to 3 hours, until wings are cooked through. Transfer wings onto 2 parchment paper-lined rimmed baking sheets. Broil for about 5 minutes, until crisp and golden. Arrange wings on a serving platter, garnished as desired. Serves 6 to 8.

Spice up your favorite ranch salad dressing. To one cup of ranch salad dressing, add 1/4 teaspoon chili powder and 1/2 teaspoon ground cumin. Let stand for 5 minutes so flavors can blend. Terrific for dipping...tasty on salads, too!

PARTY-TIME APPETIZERS

Game-Day Cheesy Chip Dip
LaDeana Cooper
Batavia, OH

An easy set-it & forget-it appetizer that will keep everyone coming back for more!

16-oz. pkg. pasteurized process cheese, cubed
Optional: 4-oz. can diced green chiles, drained

1 lb. ground Italian pork sausage, browned and drained
scoop-type tortilla chips or bread cubes

In a 2-quart crockpot, layer half each of cheese, green chiles if using and sausage; repeat layering. Cover and cook on high setting for one hour, or until cheese is beginning to melt; stir. Turn to low setting; cover and cook for another 30 minutes, or until cheese is completely melted. Stir again; serve warm with chips or bread for dipping. Serves 10 or more.

Chili Relleno Dip
Michelle Newlin
Portage, PA

A great crockpot dip to serve with tortilla chips.

8-oz. pkg. cream cheese, softened
1/4 c. ranchero or enchilada sauce
2 Anaheim or Poblano chili peppers, diced

1 t. garlic powder
1/2 t. ground cumin
Optional: 1/4 t. cayenne pepper

Mix all ingredients in a 1-1/2 quart crockpot. Cover and cook on high setting for 2 to 3 hours. Stir again; serve warm. Serves 6.

Keep a stack of shallow baskets on hand for snacking chips... just line with a napkin, add chips and serve!

CLASSIC CROCKPOT RECIPES

Hot Spiced Wine

Lynda Robson
Boston, MA

Just right for toasting the holiday season.

2 750-ml. bottles fruity red wine
2 apples, cored and quartered
2 oranges, sliced
1 lemon, sliced

1/2 c. sugar, or to taste
2 4-inch cinnamon sticks
3 whole cloves

Combine all ingredients in a 3-quart crockpot, inserting cloves in an orange slice. Cover and cook on high setting for one to 2 hours, until hot. Turn to low setting; serve warm. Makes 8 to 10 servings.

Hot Buttered Rum

Bev Traxler
British Columbia, Canada

This beverage will warm you and your guests.

1-1/2 qts. hot water
2 to 3 c. dark rum
2 c. brown sugar, packed
1/2 c. butter
3 4-inch cinnamon sticks

1 whole nutmeg, or
  1/2 t. ground nutmeg
6 whole cloves
1/8 t. salt

Combine all ingredients in a 4-quart crockpot; stir well. Cover and cook on high setting for 2 hours. Turn to low setting; continue cooking another 3 to 4 hours. Serve warm in mugs. Makes 15 to 20 servings.

May our house always be too small to hold all of our friends.
– Myrtle Reed

DELECTABLE DESSERTS

Chocolate Bread Pudding

Judy Lange
Imperial, PA

This is a great dessert for after Christmas dinner, or any special dinner...so yummy! I can put this in the crockpot, then get the rest of the meal ready and have dessert without the fuss.

6 c. day-old bread, cubed
 and divided
12-oz. pkg. semi-sweet chocolate
 chips, divided
1 c. fresh raspberries, divided
4 eggs, beaten

1/2 c. whipping cream
1/2 c. milk
1/4 c. sugar
1 t. vanilla extract
Garnish: whipped cream,
 additional raspberries

Grease the sides of a 5-quart crockpot. Add half each of bread cubes, chocolate chips and raspberries to crock. Repeat layers; set aside. In a bowl, whisk together remaining ingredients except garnish; spoon over bread mixture. Cover and cook on high setting for 2-1/2 hours. Serve topped with whipped cream and additional raspberries. Makes 8 servings.

Dollop warm desserts with fresh whipped cream...irresistible! Pour a pint of whipping cream into a deep, narrow bowl. Beat with an electric mixer on medium speed, gradually increasing to high speed, until soft peaks form. Add sugar to taste and enjoy!

DELECTABLE DESSERTS

Cherry Cobbler

Edward Kielar
Whitehouse, OH

Grandma made this with the little ones. The children loved following directions and enjoying this delicious dessert.

21-oz. can cherry pie filling
15-1/4 oz. pkg. yellow or
   white cake mix
1 egg, beaten

3 T. evaporated milk
1/2 t. cinnamon
1/2 c. chopped walnuts

Spray a 4-quart crockpot with non-stick vegetable spray; spread pie filling in bottom of crock. Cover and cook on high setting for 30 minutes. Meanwhile, in a large bowl, mix together cake mix, egg, evaporated milk and cinnamon; fold in walnuts. Spoon over hot pie filling; do not stir. Cover and cook on low setting for 2 to 3 hours, until a toothpick inserted in cake layer comes out clean. Serves 6.

Double Chocolate Pudding Cake

Marlene Burns
Cedar Rapids, IA

I love to do quick desserts in my crockpot. This is a favorite!

5.9-oz. pkg. instant chocolate
   pudding mix
3 c. milk
15-1/4 oz. pkg. chocolate fudge
   cake mix

Garnish: whipped cream
Optional: mint candies

Add dry pudding mix to a 4-quart crockpot coated with non-stick vegetable spray. Whisk in milk; set aside. Prepare cake mix according to package directions. Carefully pour batter into crock; do not stir. Cover and cook on high setting for 1-1/2 hours, or until cake is set. Serve warm with whipped cream and mint candies, if desired. Makes 12 to 14 servings.

Candy sprinkles or crushed hard candies make a fun garnish for any whipped cream-topped dessert.

CLASSIC CROCKPOT RECIPES

Aunt Margie's Apple Crisp
Carolyn Deckard
Bedford, IN

I still use my Aunt Marge's apple crisp recipe in my crockpot. It's so easy. Miss the days spent with Mom and her at the cabin on the river...such sweet memories.

4 to 5 c. Granny Smith apples,
   peeled, cored and sliced
1-1/2 c. all-purpose flour
1 c. old-fashioned oats,
   uncooked
1 c. brown sugar, packed

1/2 c. sugar
3/4 c. butter, melted
2 to 3 t. cinnamon
Garnish: vanilla ice cream or
   whipped cream

Spray a 5-quart crockpot with non-stick vegetable spray. Layer apple slices in crock; set aside. Combine remaining ingredients except garnish in a bowl; mix well and spoon over apples. Cover and cook on high setting for 3 hours, or on low setting for 4 to 6 hours, until bubbly and apples are tender. Serve topped with ice cream or whipped cream. Makes 6 servings.

Create a super cool centerpiece for a dessert party. Clean an empty ice cream tub, fill with floral foam and tuck in some bright flowers.

DELECTABLE DESSERTS

Pumpkin Pie Pudding

Ashley Jones
Gates, NC

A fall dessert that is sure to have your family & friends feeling fallish! A scrumptious end to a great meal.

15-oz. can pumpkin
12-oz. can evaporated milk
3/4 c. sugar
1/2 c. biscuit baking mix
2 eggs, beaten

2 T. butter, melted
2-1/2 t. pumpkin pie spice
2 t. vanilla extract
Garnish: whipped cream or
 vanilla ice cream

In a large bowl, combine all ingredients except garnish; mix well. Transfer to a lightly greased 4-quart crockpot. Cover and cook on low setting for 5 to 7 hours, until set. Serve warm, garnished as desired. Makes 6 to 8 servings.

Many crockpot recipes can be speeded up by cooking on high for half the time that's specified on low. For best results with crockpot baking, though, use the setting that the recipe calls for.

Blueberry-Peach Crisp

Courtney Stultz
Weir, KS

Peaches are a great summertime fruit and we love them in baked desserts. But, we tend to avoid using the oven when it is hot out. This crockpot crisp lets us enjoy a tasty treat without heating up the whole house. Don't forget to serve with ice cream!

1/3 c. plus 2 t. coconut oil or
   butter, divided
8 ripe peaches, peeled, pitted and
   thinly sliced
2 c. blueberries
1/2 c. honey, divided

2 t. cinnamon
1 t. ground ginger
2 c. all-purpose or gluten-free
   flour
1/2 t. salt

Coat a 5-quart crockpot with 2 teaspoons coconut oil or butter. Add peaches, blueberries, 1/4 cup honey and spices; toss until combined and set aside. In a small bowl, combine flour, salt, remaining honey and remaining coconut oil or butter. Stir with a fork until blended and crumbly. Sprinkle crumb mixture over fruit. Cover and cook on low setting for 2 to 3 hours. Turn off crockpot and let mixture set up before serving. Makes 10 servings.

Happiness being a dessert so sweet,
May life give you more than you can ever eat.
– Irish Toast

DELECTABLE DESSERTS

Old-Fashioned Tapioca

Emilie Britton
New Bremen, OH

This is wonderful to eat still warm or fresh from the fridge!
Great for a church supper. This makes quite a large batch...
cut the recipe in half, if you prefer.

8 c. whole milk
1 c. small tapioca pearls,
   uncooked
1-1/2 c. sugar

4 eggs, beaten
1 t. vanilla extract
Optional: whipped cream
   and/or fresh fruit

In a 5-quart crockpot, combine milk, tapioca and sugar; mix well. Cover and cook on high setting for 3 hours. In a large bowl, mix together eggs, vanilla and a little hot milk from the crockpot (this will prevent eggs from curdling). Add to crock. Cover and cook on high setting an additional 20 minutes; cover and chill. Serve garnished with whipped cream and/or fruit as desired. Makes 30 servings.

For special occasions, set out a guest book alongside
a jar of colored pens. Encourage everyone to sign it...
even small kids can draw a picture! Add favorite photos
and you'll have a cherished scrapbook in no time.

CLASSIC CROCKPOT RECIPES

Hot Fudge Sundae Cake

Vickie
Gooseberry Patch

An irresistible sweet treat that's so easy to make. We love the rich chocolate sauce that forms in the crock. Add a sprinkle of extra nuts and a maraschino cherry to each serving...yum!

1 c. all-purpose flour
1/2 c. sugar
6 T. baking cocoa, divided
2 t. baking powder
1/2 t. salt
1/2 c. milk

2 T. oil
1 t. vanilla extract
1/2 c. chopped nuts
3/4 c. brown sugar, packed
1-1/2 c. hot water
Garnish: vanilla ice cream

In a large bowl, mix flour, sugar, 2 tablespoons cocoa, baking powder and salt. Stir in milk, oil and vanilla until smooth; fold in nuts. Spread batter evenly in a greased 4-quart crockpot; set aside. In another bowl, mix brown sugar and remaining cocoa. Stir in hot water until smooth; pour evenly over batter in crock. Cover and cook on high setting for 2 to 2-1/2 hours, until a toothpick inserted in the center tests clean. Turn off crockpot; uncover and let stand for 30 to 40 minutes. Spoon warm cake into bowls. Top with a scoop of ice cream and some of the sauce from crock. Serves 6.

Take along a crockpot dessert to a party or meeting...
simply wrap it in a towel to insulate it. Serve within
an hour, or plug it in, set on low setting.

DELECTABLE DESSERTS

Black Forest Cake

Joyceann Dreibelbis
Wooster, OH

This is unbelievably easy! It combines chocolate and cherry flavors in a simple version of a dump cake that's made in a crockpot.

1/2 c. butter
8-oz. can crushed pineapple,
   drained and juice reserved
21-oz. can cherry pie filling

Optional: 1/2 c. chopped pecans
15-1/2 oz. pkg. chocolate
   cake mix

Melt butter in a small saucepan over low heat. Add reserved pineapple juice; mix well and set aside. Spread pineapple in the bottom of a 4-quart crockpot. Spoon pie filling evenly over pineapple; add chopped pecans, if desired. Sprinkle dry cake mix over pie filling. Stir butter mixture again; drizzle over cake mix. Cover and cook on low setting for about 3 hours. To serve, spoon into bowls; let cool about 5 minutes before serving. Makes 8 to 10 servings.

Serve ice cream-topped desserts to a party crowd,
the quick & easy way! Scoop ice cream ahead
of time and freeze in paper muffin liners.

199

CLASSIC CROCKPOT RECIPES

Warm Fruit Compote

Liz Plotnick-Snay
Gooseberry Patch

This dish is delightful served warm over slices of pound cake or scoops of ice cream...or all by itself! Great for a brunch buffet, too. Sometimes I add a small can of dark sweet cherries.

4-inch cinnamon stick
2 Golden Delicious apples,
  peeled, cored and sliced
1/3 c. sweetened dried
  cranberries
1/2 c. golden raisins

1/2 c. dried apricots, halved
8-oz. can pineapple tidbits in
  unsweetened juice
1/4 c. sugar
3/4 c. orange juice
21-oz. can peach pie filling

In a 3-quart crockpot, layer cinnamon stick, apples, cranberries, raisins, apricots and undrained pineapple. Sprinkle with sugar; drizzle orange juice over all. Cover and cook on low setting for 5 to 6 hours. Just before serving, stir gently; discard cinnamon stick. Gently stir in pie filling, cutting up peach slices. Serve warm. Makes 8 servings.

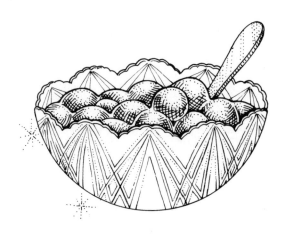

The bright colors of fresh fruit really shine in a vintage cut-glass bowl. Add a little white vinegar to the rinse water when you wash cut glass...the glass will sparkle!

DELECTABLE DESSERTS

Delicious Rice Pudding

Paula Marchesi
Auburn, PA

I always made old-fashioned rice pudding on the stovetop, the old-fashioned way, until a friend told me it's easier in the crockpot. After a few tries, I finally came up with a big hit. Now I always make it in the crockpot...it's so good!

9-1/2 c. milk, divided
1 c. long-cooking rice, uncooked
1 c. sugar
3 eggs, beaten

2 t. vanilla extract
1/4 t. salt
Optional: whipped cream,
    cinnamon or nutmeg to taste

In a 3-quart crockpot, stir together 8 cups milk, uncooked rice and sugar. Cover and cook on high setting for 3 hours. In a bowl, whisk together eggs, remaining milk, vanilla and salt. Add to crockpot and stir. Cover and cook on high setting for 25 to 30 minutes. Serve warm or cold, plain or topped with a dollop of whipped cream and a sprinkle of spice, as desired. Serves 8 to 10.

Chocolate fondue is scrumptious! Simply melt chocolate chips in a mini crockpot set on low setting. Set out dippers like pretzel rods, cubed pound cake and juicy red strawberries. Yum!

CLASSIC CROCKPOT RECIPES

Stuffed Caramel Apples

Tena Jarrell
Daniels, TN

This recipe is one of my favorites to make every fall. I love putting these apples in my crockpot before going to work. When I come home after a day of teaching, my whole house smells like baked apple pie! My son, daughter and I love topping the apples with vanilla ice cream and a drizzle of caramel sauce.

4 large tart apples
1/2 c. apple juice
1/2 c. brown sugar, packed
12 red cinnamon candies

1/4 c. butter, sliced
8 caramels, unwrapped
1/4 t. cinnamon

Core apples but leave whole; peel 3/4 inch off the top of each apple. Arrange apples in a 4-quart crockpot. Pour apple juice over apples. Fill the center of each apple with 2 tablespoons brown sugar, 3 candies, one tablespoon butter and 2 caramels. Sprinkle with cinnamon. Cover and cook on low setting for 4 to 6 hours, until apples are fork-tender. Serve warm. Makes 4 servings.

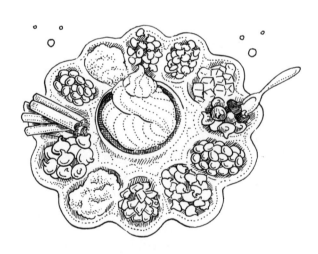

Serving coffee with a dessert buffet? Fill a deviled-egg plate with sugar cubes, mini chocolate chips, candies and other goodies for dressing up coffee.

DELECTABLE DESSERTS

Maple-Sauced Pears

Lynn Williams
Muncie, IN

Elegant and easy...perfect after a holiday dinner.

6 Bosc or Anjou pears, peeled
1/2 c. brown sugar, packed
1/3 c. pure maple syrup
1 T. butter, melted

1 t. orange zest
1/8 t. ground ginger
1 T. cornstarch
2 T. orange juice

Core pears from the bottom, leaving stems attached. Arrange pears upright in a 4-quart crockpot; set aside. In a small bowl, stir together remaining ingredients except cornstarch and orange juice; spoon over pears. Cover and cook on high setting for 2 to 2-1/2 hours, until pears are fork-tender. Remove pears from crock; place each pear in a dessert bowl and set aside. In a cup, mix cornstarch and orange juice; stir into sauce in crock. Cover and cook on high setting for about 10 minutes, until sauce is thickened. Spoon sauce over pears; serve warm. Serves 6.

Dress up dessert plates in a jiffy with a swirl of
caramel sauce, chocolate topping or maple syrup.

Apple-Pumpkin Dessert

Carol Davis
Edmond, OK

This makes the kitchen smell so wonderful when it is cooking. If you'd like a crunchy topping, crushed gingersnaps are good.

21-oz. can apple pie filling
2 c. all-purpose flour
3/4 c. brown sugar, packed
1 c. canned pumpkin
2 eggs, beaten
1/3 c. oil
2 t. baking powder

1/4 t. baking soda
1 t. cinnamon
1/2 t. ground ginger
1/2 t. nutmeg
Garnish: vanilla ice cream or
  whipped cream

Spray a 5-quart crockpot with non-stick vegetable spray. Spoon pie filling into crock; spread evenly and set aside. Combine remaining ingredients except garnish in a large bowl. Beat with an electric mixer on medium speed until blended; spoon over pie filling. Cover and cook on high setting for 1-1/2 to 2 hours, until a toothpick inserted in the center comes out clean. Immediately remove crock and set on a hot pad; cool for a few minutes. Serve topped with ice cream or whipped cream. Makes 12 servings.

For a quick dessert garnish, toast chopped nuts in a small dry skillet. Cook and stir over low heat for a few minutes, until toasty and golden. Sprinkle on warm desserts whenever you want to add a little pizzazz!

DELECTABLE DESSERTS

Campfire Baked Apples

Carolyn Deckard
Bedford, IN

My family loves fall...it's camping and apple picking season! We are lucky to live near a family-owned apple orchard. The kids always enjoy going to the orchard on a hay wagon to pick apples. Then we make delicious apple treats like this one...it's a favorite.

6 Granny Smith apples, peeled,
    halved and cored
1/4 c. butter, melted
2 T. lemon juice

1 c. brown sugar, packed
1 t. cinnamon
1/2 t. nutmeg
Garnish: vanilla ice cream

Add apples to a 5-quart crockpot. Drizzle with melted butter and lemon juice; sprinkle with brown sugar and spices. Cover and cook on low setting for 2-1/2 to 3-1/2 hours, or on high setting for 1-1/2 to 2 hours, until apples are fork-tender. Serve warm, topped with a scoop of ice cream. Makes 6 to 8 servings.

Add a touch of whimsy...use Grandma's old cow-shaped milk pitcher to top warm desserts with cream.

Country Bread Pudding

Jill Valentine
Jackson, TN

This is a great way to turn day-old bread, muffins, croissants and doughnut into something yummy! I like to keep odds & ends of leftover bread in a freezer container, then treat my family to bread pudding once I have enough. Enjoy!

8 c. bread, cubed	1/4 c. sugar
Optional: 1 c. golden raisins	1/2 t. vanilla extract
4 eggs	1/4 t. nutmeg
2 to 2-1/2 c. milk	Optional: whipping cream
1/4 c. butter, melted	

Add bread cubes to a 4-quart crockpot. Mix in raisins, if using, and set aside. Beat eggs in a large bowl; whisk in remaining ingredients except optional cream. Spoon over bread in crock; toss to coat evenly. Cover and cook on low setting for about 3 hours, until a knife tip inserted near the center tests clean. Serve warm, topped with cream, if desired. Makes 6 or more servings.

Stir up some old-fashioned hard sauce...Grandma's favorite!
Combine one cup powdered sugar, 1/4 cup softened butter,
2 teaspoons hot water and one teaspoon vanilla or rum extract.
Beat on high speed until smooth and well blended. To serve,
scoop over warm bread pudding. Keep refrigerated.

Country Peach Cobbler

LaDeana Cooper
Batavia, OH

Great for those days when you don't want the oven running, but you want that fresh-baked flavor. As with any cobbler, it is great with a scoop of your favorite vanilla ice cream! Frozen or canned sliced peaches work well, too.

4 c. ripe peaches, peeled, pitted
   and sliced
3/4 c. sugar, divided

1 c. biscuit baking mix
1 c. milk
1-1/2 t. cinnamon

In a bowl, toss peaches with 1/4 cup sugar. Transfer to a lightly greased 6-quart crockpot and set aside. In same bowl, combine biscuit mix, milk, cinnamon and remaining sugar. Stir until well blended; spoon over peaches. Cover and cook on low setting for 3 hours, or until set in the center. Serve warm. Makes 6 or more servings.

Stir up sweet memories...look through Grandma's recipe box
and rediscover a long-forgotten favorite dessert recipe
to share with your family.

CLASSIC CROCKPOT RECIPES

Apple Brown Betty

Samantha Starks
Madison, WI

A splendid old-fashioned dessert. My grandmother used to bake it in her oven...now I fix it & forget it in my crockpot. A drizzle of caramel syrup is a must!

6 c. Granny Smith apples, peeled,
   cored and sliced
1 c. sugar
1 T. all-purpose flour

1 t. cinnamon
zest and juice of 1 lemon
3 c. soft bread crumbs
1/2 c. butter, melted

In a large bowl, combine apples, sugar, flour, cinnamon, lemon zest and juice. Toss to coat well; set aside. In another bowl, toss together bread crumbs and melted butter. In a lightly greased 5-quart crockpot, layer 1/3 of bread crumb mixture and 1/2 of apple mixture. Repeat layering twice, with remaining bread crumbs on top. Cover and cook on high setting for 4 hours, or until bubbly, golden and apples are tender. Makes 6 servings.

Create a heavenly glaze for apple desserts. Melt together 1/2 cup butterscotch chips, 2 tablespoons butter and 2 tablespoons whipping cream over low heat.

DELECTABLE DESSERTS

Berry Patch Compote

Mary Hughes
Talladega, AL

A luscious dessert, spooned over ice cream...or treat everyone to warm berries over French toast for breakfast!

6 c. frozen mixed berries	1/4 c. orange juice
1/2 c. sugar, or more to taste	2 T. cornstarch
1-1/2 t. orange zest	2 T. water

In a 4-quart crockpot, stir together frozen berries, sugar, orange zest and juice. Cover and cook on high setting for about 1-1/2 hours, until hot and bubbly. Stir together cornstarch and water in a cup until dissolved; stir into berry mixture. Cover again and cook until thickened, 5 to 10 minutes. Serve warm or at room temperature. Makes 6 servings.

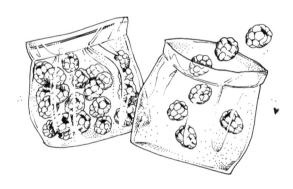

Enjoy fresh berries throughout the year...freeze them during berry season! Spread ripe berries in a single layer on a baking sheet and freeze until solid, then store them in plastic freezer bags. Later, you can pour out just the amount you need.

CLASSIC CROCKPOT RECIPES

Big Easy Bananas Foster
Darrell Lawry
Kissimmee, FL

After I'd tried Bananas Foster on a trip to New Orleans, I knew
I had to have it again! This recipe is scrumptious over
ice cream, crepes or pound cake.

1/2 to 3/4 c. brown sugar,
   packed
1/2 c. butter, sliced
1/4 t. cinnamon

4 ripe bananas, cut into
   1-inch chunks
2 to 3 T. dark rum

Combine brown sugar, butter and cinnamon in a 3-quart crockpot.
Cover and cook on low setting for 30 to 60 minutes, stirring once or
twice, until butter is melted and sugar is dissolved. Add bananas,
stirring gently to coat; stir in rum. Cover and continue cooking for
15 to 20 minutes, until bananas are warm. Makes 4 servings.

Minister's Delight
Sharon Tillman
Hampton, VA

This dessert is so easy to put together...such a comforting dish!
Make it with your favorite fruit filling and top with ice cream.

15-1/4 oz. pkg. yellow cake mix
21-oz. can apple, cherry or peach
   pie filling

1/2 c. butter, melted
Optional: 1/3 c. chopped walnuts

Spray a 4-quart crockpot with non-stick vegetable spray; spoon pie
filling evenly into crock. Combine dry cake mix and butter in a bowl;
mixture will be crumbly. Sprinkle over pie filling. Sprinkle with walnuts,
if desired. Cover and cook on low setting for 2 to 3 hours. Serve warm.
Serves 6.

Add a touch of sweetness...serve special desserts
in Grandma's treasured dessert bowls.

DELECTABLE DESSERTS

Caramel Apple Dump Cake

*Tina Matie
Alma, GA*

This delicious dessert is perfect for fall celebrations. It's my favorite for Thanksgiving and Christmas. Serve it with whipped cream or cinnamon ice cream for an even more decadent dessert.

20-oz. can apple pie filling
1/2 c. caramel syrup

15-1/4 oz. pkg. yellow cake mix
1/2 c. butter, melted

Generously spray a 6-quart crockpot with non-stick vegetable spray. Spoon pie filling into crock; spread evenly in the bottom. Drizzle with caramel syrup; set aside. In a bowl, combine dry cake mix and melted butter; stir together until crumbly. Spoon over mixture in crockpot; spread evenly. Cover and cook on high setting for 2 hours, or on low setting for 4 hours. Serve warm. Serves 12.

Gramma's Baked Custard

*Tonya Sheppard
Galveston, TX*

Cozy and comforting...just like Gramma used to make for me! If you don't have a trivet, balls of aluminum foil will work.

3 eggs, lightly beaten
1/3 c. sugar
1 t. vanilla extract

2 c. whole milk
1/4 t. nutmeg

Grease a 1-1/2 quart casserole dish that fits inside your crockpot; set aside. Set a trivet in crockpot. Add 1-1/2 to 2 cups of hot water to crock; set aside. In a bowl, whisk together eggs, sugar, vanilla and milk; pour into dish. Sprinkle with nutmeg. Cover dish tightly with foil; set on trivet in crock. Cover and cook on high setting for 2 to 3 hours, until custard is firm. Serve warm or chilled. Serves 4.

For delicious flavor in desserts, freshly grated nutmeg can't be beat!

CLASSIC CROCKPOT RECIPES

Merlot Spiced Apples

Courtney Stultz
Weir, KS

The crockpot is great for more than just main dishes. These easy apples are yummy served with ice cream or fresh whipped cream!

1 T. coconut oil
1/2 c. Merlot or other red wine,
   or apple juice
1/4 c. sugar
1 T. all-purpose flour
1 T. cinnamon

1 t. apple pie spice
4 Golden Delicious or Honeycrisp
   apples, peeled, cored and
   thinly sliced
1 orange, sectioned
1/2 c. chopped walnuts or pecans

Add oil to a 5-quart crockpot turned to high setting and set aside. In a small bowl, combine wine or juice, sugar, flour and spices; stir until well combined. Add apples, orange and nuts; stir until well coated and add to crockpot. Cover and cook on high setting for one hour, stirring 4 to 5 times, or until apples are fork-tender. Let cool about 10 minutes to allow sauce to thicken. Makes 6 servings.

Before chopping nuts in a food processor, dust them with flour or powdered sugar...they'll chop easily and won't stick to the blades!

DELECTABLE DESSERTS

Gingerbread Pudding Cake
Liz Blackstone
Racine, WI

I love to make crockpot desserts for all our family get-togethers. Was happy to discover this recipe that's perfect for Christmastime! I top it with a sprinkle of chopped, candied ginger.

14-1/2 oz. pkg. gingerbread mix
1/2 c. milk
1/2 c. raisins
2-1/4 c. water

3/4 c. brown sugar, packed
3/4 c. butter, sliced
Optional: vanilla ice cream

In a large bowl, combine dry gingerbread mix and milk; stir until moistened. Fold in raisins; batter will be thick. Spread batter evenly in the bottom of a 4-quart crockpot coated with non-stick vegetable spray; set aside. In a saucepan, combine water, brown sugar and butter. Bring to a boil over medium-high heat; reduce heat. Boil gently for 2 minutes. Carefully pour over batter. Cover and cook on high setting for 2 hours, until set. (Center may appear moist, but will set up as it cools.) Turn off crockpot; uncover and let stand for 45 minutes to cool slightly before serving. To serve, spoon warm cake into dessert bowls. If desired, serve topped with a scoop of ice cream. Serves 8.

Crockpot desserts are perfect for open-house buffets... guests can help themselves to a warm dessert whenever they're ready for it.

CLASSIC CROCKPOT RECIPES

Applesauce Spice Cake

Nola Coons
Gooseberry Patch

The delicious smells of apples and spices wafting through the house are reason enough to make this cake! It's wonderful for fall get-togethers.

2 c. all-purpose flour
1 t. baking soda
1/8 t. salt
1-1/2 t. ground ginger
1 t. cinnamon
1/4 t. ground cloves
1/2 c. butter, softened

1/2 c. sugar
1/2 c. dark brown sugar, packed
2 eggs
1 c. unsweetened applesauce
1 t. vanilla extract
Garnish: powdered sugar

Press a 15-inch square of parchment paper into a 5-quart crockpot, allowing any excess to come up the sides. Set aside. In a large bowl, whisk together flour, baking soda, salt and spices; set aside. In another large bowl, beat butter and sugars with an electric mixer on medium speed for about 3 minutes, until light and fluffy. Beat in eggs, one at a time; beat in applesauce and vanilla. (Mixture will look curdled.) Turn mixer speed to low. Gradually beat in flour mixture, just until blended. Transfer batter to crockpot. Cover and cook on high setting for 2 to 2-1/2 hours, until set and a toothpick inserted in the center tests clean. Using the parchment paper as handles, lift cake to a wire rack; let cool for at least 15 minutes. Cut into wedges; dust with powdered sugar and serve. Makes 10 servings.

Don't tuck Grandma's beautiful cake plates away, saving them for "someday." Get them out and enjoy them now! Each time they're used, they'll be a sweet reminder of her homemade treats.

DELECTABLE DESSERTS

Country Pear Crisp

Amy Butcher
Columbus, GA

Perfect after a visit to our neighborhood farmers' market!
Sometimes I like to double all the ingredients except the pears
to make more of the yummy crisp topping.

4 ripe Anjou pears, peeled, cored
   and diced
1/4 c. butter, room temperature
1/2 c. brown sugar, packed
1/4 c. sugar

1 t. cinnamon
1 t. vanilla extract
1 c. old-fashioned oats,
   uncooked
Garnish: vanilla ice cream

Spread pears in a a 4-quart crock pot; set aside. In a bowl, stir together butter and sugars. Add cinnamon and vanilla; mix well. Stir in oats until mixture is crumbly. Spread oat mixture evenly over pears. Cover and cook on low setting for 4 hours, or on high setting for 2 hours, until bubbly and pears are tender. Serve with a scoop of ice cream. Makes 6 servings.

Add a tasty, crunchy topping to crockpot fruit desserts...
try finely crushed vanilla wafers or gingerbread cookies,
even pretzels for a sweet & salty taste.

Sweet Candied Nuts

Norma Burton
Kuna, ID

My sister shared this recipe with me when I needed a gift for my neighbors at Christmas. The nuts were a big hit, and the glass jars looked so pretty decorated with colorful ribbon and festive greenery.

2 c. pecan halves
2 c. walnut halves
2 c. whole almonds
1 egg white, beaten
1 T. vanilla extract
1 c. sugar

1 c. brown sugar, packed
2 T. cinnamon
1/2 t. nutmeg
1/2 t. ground ginger
1/8 t. salt
1/4 c. water

Coat a 4-quart crockpot with non-stick vegetable spray. Add all nuts; toss to mix and set aside. In a small bowl, whisk egg white with vanilla. Spoon over nuts; toss together. In a separate bowl, mix together remaining ingredients except water. Pour over nuts; stir to coat well. Cover and cook on low setting for 3 hours, stirring every 20 minutes to prevent burning; stir in water during the last 20 minutes. Spread nuts evenly on an aluminum foil-lined rimmed baking sheet; allow to cool. Break apart nuts; store in covered containers. Makes about 6 cups.

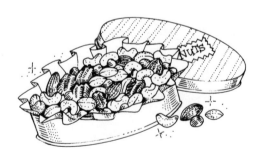

Give a gift of candied nuts in a good-as-new thrift-store tin...just line with parchment paper and fill! It's an extra gift for the lucky recipient.

DELECTABLE DESSERTS

Peanut Cluster Candies
Brittany Crawford
Newbern, TN

I make these goodies for my grandchildren every Christmas. They never last long! Make them extra special with candy sprinkles.

12-oz. pkg. semi-sweet
   chocolate chips
12-oz. pkg. milk chocolate chips
12-oz. pkg. peanut butter chips

24-oz. pkg. white melting
   chocolate, unwrapped
2 16-oz. jars lightly salted
   roasted peanuts

In a 6-quart crockpot, layer all chips, then white chocolate block; spread peanuts on top. Cover and cook on low setting for one hour, stirring every 15 minutes, or until chocolate is melted and smooth. Drop mixture by tablespoonfuls onto a rimmed baking sheet. Cover and chill for 20 to 30 minutes; store candies in an airtight container. Makes 4 to 5 dozen.

Brenda's Nutty Fudge
Deb Dunham
Lumberton, TX

Our cousin Brenda had these candies on hand for holiday visitors. So great with a cup of hot coffee! I began to make them myself for gifts and for parties.

12-oz. pkg. chopped pecans
   or walnuts
6-oz. pkg. semi-sweet
   chocolate chips

12-oz. pkg. white chocolate chips
24-oz. pkg. white melting
   chocolate, unwrapped

Spray a 5-quart crockpot with non-stick vegetable spray. Evenly layer nuts and chocolate chips in crock; top with white chocolate block. Cover and cook on low setting for one to 2 hours. Turn off crockpot; stir very well. Drop mixture by teaspoonfuls onto a wax paper-lined rimmed baking sheet. Let cool at least one hour. Store in plastic freezer bags or an airtight container. Makes 1-1/2 to 2 dozen.

INDEX

INDEX

INDEX

Find Gooseberry Patch
wherever you are!

www.gooseberrypatch.com

Call us toll-free at 1·800·854·6673

more time for fun   the perfect meal

oh-so easy

slowly simmered

flavorful favorites

'round the table

home cooking   sweet & savory

U.S. to Metric Recipe Equivalents

Volume Measurements

1/4 teaspoon	1 mL
1/2 teaspoon	2 mL
1 teaspoon	5 mL
1 tablespoon = 3 teaspoons	15 mL
2 tablespoons = 1 fluid ounce	30 mL
1/4 cup	60 mL
1/3 cup	75 mL
1/2 cup = 4 fluid ounces	125 mL
1 cup = 8 fluid ounces	250 mL
2 cups = 1 pint =16 fluid ounces	500 mL
4 cups = 1 quart	1 L

Weights

1 ounce	30 g
4 ounces	120 g
8 ounces	225 g
16 ounces = 1 pound	450 g

Oven Temperatures

300° F	150° C
325° F	160° C
350° F	180° C
375° F	190° C
400° F	200° C
450° F	230° C

Baking Pan Sizes

Square		*Loaf*	
8x8x2 inches	2 L = 20x20x5 cm	9x5x3 inches	2 L = 23x13x7 cm
9x9x2 inches	2.5 L = 23x23x5 cm	*Round*	
Rectangular		8x1-1/2 inches	1.2 L = 20x4 cm
13x9x2 inches	3.5 L = 33x23x5 cm	9x1-1/2 inches	1.5 L = 23x4 cm